Guns, Books and Lawsuits

Guns, Books and Lawsuits

A Memoir

DR. ROBERT KIMBALL

LIEUTENANT COLONEL, U.S. ARMY RETIRED

authorHOUSE®

AuthorHouse™
1663 Liberty Drive
Bloomington, IN 47403
www.authorhouse.com
Phone: 1-800-839-8640

First published by AuthorHouse   07/16/2011

ISBN: 978-1-4634-3177-8 (sc)
ISBN: 978-1-4634-3180-8 (ebk)

Library of Congress Control Number: 2011911679

Printed in the United States of America

To Jim, Kathryn
Nicole, Cameron, Jami
And Kori

ACKNOWLEDGEMENTS

Vyone Kimball, my wife of almost 45 years, was my full partner in writing this memoir. For almost six months we reviewed memories, edited the manuscript, and located pictures to help readers appreciate the memoir. However, I alone am responsible for the contents of this Memoir.

This memoir would not have been written if Rosemary Covalt had not badgered me for 10 years to write it. I would never have attended college and gained the skills to write if Robert Johnson had not educated me on achieving a higher education and encouraged me to pursue it in 1964.

My military career would have ended abruptly in 1973, if Lieutenant General Marc Cisneros (U.S. Army, Retired) had followed orders from his superior to end my career. As a result of his support throughout my military career, I was selected for one of the highest honors in the Army, to command a combat arms battalion.

I owe LULAC Council 402 (League of Latin American Citizens) members my eternal gratitude for supporting me and my causes when Houston Independent School District retaliated against me for blowing the whistle on falsified dropout rates in the district. I especially want to thank Mary Almendarez, Edward Ybarra and Rosemary Covalt for their unwavering support during those difficult days. I also want to thank Robert Covalt for allowing his wife to spend hundreds of stressful hours advocating for me during those turbulent times.

My grandchildren, Nicole, Cameron, Jami and Kori's questions motivated me to write a memoir, to help them learn about their grandfather's experiences in the last century and to someday share them with their children.

FOREWARD

As I learned during my 35 year military service; which included service in Vietnam, Jonestown Massacre, and Panama operation Just Cause, and subsequently in academia, there are times when you have to make a choice between what is easy, and what is right. As you'll soon read, Lieutenant Colonel Bob Kimball found himself in similar situations many times in the military and as a civilian, and he always made what to him was the right decision. It was not necessarily the decision his superiors desired. When I met him in 1974 as a young Captain, he quickly made an impression on me as a man of integrity.

This memoir covers his early childhood where he faced adversity in the form of poverty, ridicule, and discrimination. It did not matter to him that he was poor or that his mother was illiterate. He just knew he wanted to succeed in life, unlike his alcoholic father who died when Bob was only nine, leaving 11 children. If he didn't know how to do something or have the money to get what he wanted, he read about it or earned the money by selling newspapers in front of the Nashua, NH, factories. There are not too many nine-year-olds who have bought the family's first television or piano. No matter what the odds, he would get the job done, both as a child and then as an adult who faced many family and personal challenges. Everyone who was not born with a silver spoon in their mouth should read this journey of Bob Kimball.

In spite of being a high school dropout, Bob learned as much as he could in his early Army years as an enlisted man about career opportunities and the various paths to success. The reader will learn how he completed years of education in a short period of time leading to a Doctorate degree in spite of being a high school dropout. Education was always of the utmost importance to him. With knowledge and persistence, he learned that he could accomplish his goals, serve his country and help those who felt powerless.

Bob married young, but that didn't stop him from continuing his education, taking care of his family and serving in the Army a second time, this time as an officer volunteering for two tours in Vietnam. He carried out all the duties demanded of an officer, but he was always there for his wife and children. Their needs were always in the forefront of his mind. After more training and education he went on to serve in Europe and eventually commanded a battalion as his final Army career assignment.

After serving in the military, Bob moved into the education sector, (as did I, serving as President of the University of Texas-Kingsville for three years) where he continue to put his principles (truth, justice and equality) before all other things, including moving up the career ladder. As the reader will see, he worked in many areas of education, including teaching, administration, and training graduate students in the how's and why's of becoming a successful school administrator.

Upon his retirement in education, the reader will learn how his perseverance continued in working for the rights of minorities, standing up for the rights of students, and challenging school authorities to properly report accurate school dropout numbers and to stop pushing young students out of the educational system. The work I've done with the Kenedy Foundation, supporting many deserving charities is something I'll always be proud of. I think of Bob's actions in serving as an advocate for minorities and the powerless in the same way, except that instead of recognition and thanks, he often was persecuted or faced legal action as a result of his advocacy.

In this memoir some names have been changed for obvious reasons, but the descriptions are accurate. Bob has been encouraging me to write a memoir of my own. I know it is probably the right thing to do for my family and others, but it certainly will not be easy.

Marc Cisneros, Lieutenant General, U.S. Army Retired

CONTENTS

CHAPTER ONE

A Ghetto Education and Emancipation
(1944-1961)

Most poor people never become aware that they were born powerless and are more than likely to experience powerless lives. Poor people quickly learn that the most important things in life are simply food, shelter and clothing. The only power they understand is the power necessary to survive poverty. In Nashua, New Hampshire, when I was born, few poor people voted, because they could not afford the poll tax.

The poll tax was required to be paid for anyone who wanted to vote for President or any public office official. Paying the poll tax and voting did not put food on the table or pay the rent. Living in poverty would make my life as an adult simple in many ways. It would teach me to live with less than the bare necessities, avoid greed, tolerate hardships, and the consequences of discrimination.

On occasion, our family was denied the use of the public swimming pool. Teachers branded us as "poor white trash" and "failures" because we did not take school seriously, wore dirty clothes, and were often in trouble with the law. Police officers often visited our home to arrest family members. We had few reasons to smile, laugh or be happy growing up. We were provided only enough food to sustain life, and enough clothing and shelter to protect us from the elements. Only one of my parents' twelve children graduated from high school.

When you are poor, you adjust to being underprivileged and life seems normal. Until the age of 10, I never had an opportunity to visit a house. We always resided in run down apartments scheduled for demolition. Later, when I did visit a house, I was surprised when I observed furniture placed in the yard. Our apartment had very little furniture, and to learn that some people had enough furniture to place some in the yard was a major life discovery for me. In the early 1950's, I had no way of knowing there were different lifestyles that existed outside of our own. As poor people, our family stood out from others because at that time few families in New Hampshire were categorized as poor.

When I was born in 1944, most of the residents in Nashua were employed in the field of manufacturing. There were shoe, plastics, rubber and other factories in the city that would employ residents despite their lack of education, especially during the war years. However, in the early 1940s my father was a convicted felon who had served two years of a five year prison sentence for attempted sexual contact with his 14-year-old niece. As a poorly educated ex-convict, and an alcoholic he had difficulty finding and keeping a job.

The total bill for the hospital and doctor's fees related to my birth in December 1944 was only $50.00. The bill was paid in full on the day my mother was released from St. Joseph Hospital in Nashua. My mother had recently received the proceeds of an insurance policy upon the death of her brother Robert in October 1944. He lived with our family until he died at the early age of 24, two months before my birth. I was given his first name and my middle name came from my mother's uncle Harry.

My father, Leslie Morton Kimball, was born in Framingham, Massachusetts, on December 9, 1889. His father Marcus, (1859), grandfather Joseph, (1817), great grandfather, Joseph, (1785) and great great grandfather John (1731) were all born in New Hampshire. They were all farmers until the industrial revolution caught up with them in the 1880s. My grandfather Marcus moved to Massachusetts because of the many manufacturing jobs available there. He found a job working in the shoe manufacturing business. When my father was born, there were few public schools and many children quit school to go to work in the factories by the age of fifteen.

In 1895, six years after my father was born, his mother, Ellen, died at age 31 from pneumonia. His father Marcus remarried and returned to New Hampshire, where he lived until his death in October 1944. Leslie was one of five children born to Marcus and Ellen. In 1907, when Leslie was 18 he married Mary Blanchard, who at 36, was twice his age. She bore no children during the marriage. They were married for about 15 years when she passed away.

In 1931 at the age of 41, Leslie traveled to Lexington, Virginia in a Model T Ford with his brother, Oliver, and Oliver's wife, Annie, to visit Annie's family. There he met Annie's cousin, Nancy (Nannie) May Smith, who was 17 (24 years younger than Leslie). Nannie would eventually become Leslie's wife and my mother. Nannie had never attended school and was illiterate, as were her parents, as well as her paternal grandparents.

Nannie was the first of six children born in Virginia to John Harvey (1888) and Elizabeth (Lizzie) Smith (1892), who had married in 1910. John, who went by his middle name of Harvey, was one of seven children, born to Andrew (1850) and Polly Smith (1853). The Smiths were all born in Virginia or West Virginia.

John Harvey Smith registered for the military draft in 1917 and again in 1942. However, his draft registration form reveals that he misrepresented his family in 1917 so that he would not be drafted. His registration card stated that he had nine children, when in fact, according to the 1920 census; he had only three at the most.

My grandmother was a Native American Indian, whose parents were most likely from the Monacan group of Indians in Virginia. My grandfather helped her escape from a hostile environment in West Virginia. In 1914, in Virginia, the director of Vital Statistics directed that birth certificates for all Indians be changed to reflect their race as colored. In 1924, the Virginia law was again clarified in the "Racial Integrity Act". The act criminalized marriages between whites and coloreds; and legally classified Indians as colored. This law was not declared unconstitutional until 1967, by the Supreme Court of the United States in Loving vs. Virginia.

At the time of the 1910 U.S. census, my grandmother Lizzie was living with her husband's family. She was falsely listed as a daughter, and my grandfather John, as a son-in-law in the household of Andrew and Polly Smith; to conceal the fact that she was a Native American Indian. Actually, John was Andrew's son and Lizzie was John's wife. Little is known about my grandmother. Her death certificate revealed that her father's name and mother's maiden name were not obtainable. Unfortunately, she was killed crossing a highway by an automobile on October 20, 1956.

My grandparents were share croppers. They were given permission to occupy a dilapidated cabin in exchange for helping with the land owner's crops.

On his trip to Lexington in 1931, Leslie offered to take Nannie to live with her cousin, Annie Smith, who lived in New Hampshire with her husband Oliver, Leslie's brother. Her father objected and refused to give his permission. Nannie was insistent and got into an argument with her father while standing on a bridge overlooking a deep gorge. She threatened to jump off the bridge and kill herself if he did not let her go. Her father agreed to let her travel to New Hampshire with Leslie. On July 19 1931, she married Leslie and on August 6, 1932, they had the first of their 12 children, Annabelle (Trudy). Trudy was followed by Martha (Marti), June 15, 1934, Leslie (Buddy), October 2, 1935, Charles, May 1, 1937, Fredrick (Fred), April 12, 1938, Patrick (Pat), March 17, 1940 and Shirley, November 11, 1941 who died in childbirth.

In late 1941 my father was sentenced to serve five years in the state prison system. He had pleaded guilty to attempted rape of his niece, Mabel Kimball, who was 14 years old at the time. In a photo of him taken in prison he has a sign in front of his chest that read: "incest". At the time of his incarceration he had fathered seven children during 10 years of marriage.

While my mother was in labor with the seventh child, Shirley Agnes, she was informed that her husband had been arrested, which may have caused the child to be stillborn. The state authorities decided to remove all the children from the home and place them in foster homes, because the head of the household was incarcerated and my mother was unable to provide for the children.

Nannie told everyone she would do whatever it took to get her children back. She found work as a housekeeper and within three years, she had succeeded in having her six children returned to her. My father sent her many love letters[1] from prison, expecting to join her when he was released. On May 9, 1943, he was released from prison early on good behavior and immediately impregnated my mother. She bore her eighth child two months premature on January 11, 1944. They named the girl Shirley Agnes after the baby they had lost.

The death of Robert F. Smith, my mother's brother, in our apartment in October 1944, at the age of 24 was reported as an accident. However, there is a possibility he may have been killed by my father. My father was often intoxicated and insanely jealous of anyone who spent time with his wife. On the night of his death, Robert attended a movie with my mother.

After returning from the movie, my mother went to her third floor bedroom and heard a loud noise downstairs. She went down to the second level to investigate and discovered her brother Robert, lying dead at the bottom of the stairs. My father had a reputation for initiating a fight at the slightest provocation. He stood less than five feet tall, had a small body frame and was often the one to leave a fight in worse shape.

My father walked a mile to a phone booth and called for an ambulance. When he reported the incident he was still on parole for the felony he had committed in 1941. He could not afford any problems with his parole status so reported it as an accident. Obviously, my mother did not want to lose her children or husband again so most likely chose to remain silent when the police arrived, and a few months later, on December 21, 1944, I was born.

Leslie found keeping a job even more difficult after WWII. He moved from job to job and was often unemployed, which

---

[1]   A copy of one of his letters is in appendix B.

made him unable to provide for the basic needs of his growing family.

My father spent most of his time at the neighborhood bars and usually returned home intoxicated. I can recall him coming home intoxicated and being hidden under a bed by my two older sisters, Trudy and Marti, when I was about five years old. I watched as the two teenage girls stood at the top of the stairs and attempted to protect our father from some men who had chased him home, by waving brooms and yelling at them to go away.

On another occasion, when I was about six years old, he came home intoxicated and caused several of us to get scalded with hot water. Because there was no functioning bathtub in the apartment, my mother would heat a tub of water on the wood stove so she could bathe us. My father came home angry and tipped the tub over which caused the hot water to spill on our naked bodies and burn our tender skin. My father often beat his older sons with belts, switches and his fists. A year after I was born, my brother Daniel (Danny) was born on December 16, 1945. He was soon followed by Nancy, July 11, 1947 and Larry, January 26, 1949.

We had a lot of visitors to our apartment, especially aunts, uncles and cousins. Two of my mother's sisters had prostituted themselves in the local area during the depression and a few cousins behaved like sexual perverts. On one occasion, when I was about six, I woke up in bed to find that my naked 20-year-old cousin Morris Kimball, the son of Oliver Kimball, had placed my hand on his genitals. I became alarmed and ran from the bedroom at our apartment on Canal Street. Morris was the brother of Mabel Kimball who my father admitted to attempting to rape. One of the disadvantages of growing up poor in a large family is that you are at greater risk of becoming a victim of sexual, physical, and mental abuse.

When my father was not working, which was most of the time in the 1940's and early 1950's, he would often visit a wooded area in downtown Nashua called "The Jungle" and sit by a river with other alcoholics to drink beer. One day, I went there with my brothers Pat and Danny to throw rocks at the alcoholics until we realized we were throwing rocks at our own father.

After World War II, my father suffered more from the effects of his alcoholism and found it impossible to take care of the needs of his very large family. In 1945, he was an ex-convict with nine children at fifty-six years old. As a consequence, our family lived in absolute poverty. We suffered from malnutrition and were often ill. My brother Danny was diagnosed with rickets, a disease caused by malnutrition.

We wore oversized hand-me-downs and clothes other people threw away. We went to school dirty and hungry. In the 1st grade, I chewed pencils for nourishment in class and even tried white chalk. While in the 2nd grade, I had the one and only dental procedure of my childhood, which resulted in the inside of my mouth being numbed. During class, I chewed on the inside walls of my mouth to relieve my hunger. After the numbness wore off, the damage I had done left me in quite a lot of pain.

Our single daily meal usually consisted solely of potatoes. My parents bought a 50 pound bag of potatoes almost every week. Any other foods they provided were kept from spoiling by placing them in an ice box. Once every few days, a truck would deliver ice for the ice box. On rare occasions, we had fried salt pork. Salt pork is a slab of fat from the pig and is usually used for seasoning. However, my mother would fry it like bacon on the wood stove and we would devour it. On other rare occasions, she would fry tripe, the inside of a cow's stomach, and this became a very special treat for us. Salt pork and tripe cost pennies a pound back in the early 1950's. A few times a year, my father would go fishing in a polluted river that contained raw sewage. Sometimes he came home with ten to fifteen large catfish and would place them, still alive, in the same tub where we were bathed, until my mother could prepare them for dinner.

For the first seven years of my life, we lived in an apartment on the third floor, above a market on Canal Street in Nashua, which was near several bars that served only beer. I was a sickly child and suffered from the whooping cough and other illnesses. Most of us suffered from poor health due to the lack of proper food and the turmoil caused by an extended family of alcoholics.

On August 3, 1950, my sister Nancy, who had just turned three, fell from one of the windows of our third story apartment because the windows had no screens and she was not being properly supervised. She suffered a severe head injury that placed her in a coma for about six months. Nancy was not expected to live, but she did survive the accident. A portion of her brain had to be removed due to the severe damage caused by her fall. Later in life she would also be struck down in two separate automobile accidents. Nancy survived all those injuries but would be mentally challenged for the rest of her life. Poor health and accidents are among the hazards of which families living in poverty face an elevated risk.

In 1951, first my sister, Trudy, and then my brother Charles, left home to join the Air Force.

I had turned six in December the previous year, but was not old enough to begin school until September 1951. My first school, Temple Street School, was housed in one building that was built of brick and three stories high. In order to travel to the school, we had to cross railroad tracks, go through the woods, and cross a foot bridge over the Nashua River. We could save some time by climbing a rock wall and going through someone's yard, which we did when we were running late. We always went to school hungry, dirty and wearing unwashed clothes that were too big or too small. My 1st grade teacher was an elderly lady, Ms. Antoine, who often put her head on her desk and cried because she hated her job and her students so much.

When I was seven, in 1952, we moved into a smaller apartment above another market, and my father began receiving counseling from a pastor regarding his alcoholism. He did not stop drinking beer, but he did spend less time at the bars and more time at home. We soon found ourselves unwelcome at the apartment and moved again, in January 1954, to one of many apartments in a row of apartments at 23 School Street. The rent was very affordable, only $5.50 a week! The apartment had three levels and about 10 rooms. Soon after moving to

School Street, my father found a job as a dish washer in a restaurant that paid 60 cents per hour.

In late 1954, he became ill with pneumonia. Like most poor people, he did not like going to a doctor because a visit required funds that were in limited supply in our home. He refused the family's demand that he visit a doctor and his condition worsened. Finally, a doctor was called to the apartment, at which time he was sent to the hospital. However, it was too late; he passed away at the hospital before they could find him a bed. My understanding is that because he was poor, the hospital did not want to assign him a room and decided to leave him in the hallway until he passed. When I learned of his death, I cried for the first time in my life that I could remember.

I have no recollection of having any communication with my father in almost ten years that I lived with him. I remember the previously mentioned incidents involving him. I also recall him smoking a lot and when he was home, he would listen with an ear close to the radio playing with the buttons on his shirt.

The word "love" was never used in my home by anyone. I never observed my parents or my brothers and sisters hug each other. Other than being angry with each other all the time, everyone in our family was emotionally detached from each other. There was no attempt to manage anger in the home. Some of my brothers became so angry at each other that they attempted to kill each other. My brother Charles became so angry he said he wanted to kill Fred. Danny cut my arm with a razor blade. We could not afford a doctor so there were no stitches and consequently a large scar remains to this day. He also attacked me with a knife twice before we were 12 years old. He continued expressing his hatred of me and our other siblings during his lifetime.

My first few years of school were uneventful, except for hunger, and the discrimination demonstrated by my classmates and teachers because of my poverty. My father, mother or older siblings never visited my schools in their lifetimes. They never encouraged education. They never said, "Do you have homework", or asked what happened at school. If we did not want to go to school, we were not forced to go. There were no questions from any family member if we decided to skip school. While I was in the 3rd grade, I experienced stomach pains and was rushed to the hospital. No one told me why I was going or what was going to happen to me at the hospital. I was sent into the operating room without any explanation. I was given gas to put me to sleep, which was a horrifying experience. As it turned out, I had an operation to remove my appendix.

After beginning the 4th grade, life in our home did change somewhat. When my father passed away my mother began receiving monthly checks from Social Security and received additional help from the community. Clothes were donated to us from a church. A church family who had just returned from a visit to Texas donated some western boots to our family.

I wore them to school because I had no other shoes to wear. Wearing those boots caused me to be bullied even more than usual. Since my mother could not read, she always insisted that I go grocery shopping with her. She had me keep track of her purchases and the cost of the groceries in her shopping cart. She did not want to be embarrassed at the checkout by not having enough money.

Teachers at Temple Street School never encouraged me nor made any physical contact with me until the 5th grade. We sensed that they detested us because we frequently arrived at school with head lice and our clothes and bodies were often dirty. My older brothers who had preceded us had serious discipline records at school, which reflected on us, the younger siblings. When I was about to begin the 5th grade, I was told by other students not to go to Ms. Bessie Theros' class because she was really "mean". There were only two 5th grade teachers. After I reported to the teacher who I was told was not mean, Ms. Theros came into the classroom and escorted me to her room.

As luck would have it, this teacher turned out to be the cause of a major turning point in my outlook on education and life. As she led me out of the classroom, she put her arm around me and told me we were going to have a lot of fun in her classroom. It was the first time I could ever remember someone putting their arm around me. She hugged me several times with great sincerity as we walked to her classroom. I will never forget that moment as it was the time I first felt a sense that someone cared about me as an individual. Up to that time, I did not like school or teachers. Ms. Theros, my 5th grade teacher, instilled in me the desire to be a lifelong learner. Later, she would become an outstanding school principal.

Ms. Theros gave us assignments that required us to go to the city library. I had never visited a library before. There I fell in love with reading. The public library in Nashua sits on a hill overlooking downtown. There was a large section of books in the library for young readers, which included many biographies. I read several, and they gave me an appreciation for the character of great leaders and inspired me to learn more about leadership.

In the following years, I sought out books that discussed military operations and the significance of tactics and strategy. My interest in the military, at such a young age, would eventually lead me to a career in the military.

Unfortunately, I was not able to visit the library every day after school because I had to work at my job selling newspapers. I was very successful at selling newspapers. I started when I was six years old and continued until I was fifteen years old. Each day, after school, I would go to the office of the Telegraph, and pick up a large white bag filled with newspapers. The bag had a strap, which I would brace on my head and then carry to the factories to sell the papers. I had to walk up a large hill with this heavy load. I had to bend forward so that all I could see was the ground. It was especially difficult during the winter months, when I had to walk up the steep hill covered with snow and ice.

At the factories, I would arrive before the employees were released from work. As they rushed pass me, I would yell, "Telegraph, Telegraph, Telegraph". I always sold all of my papers and received lots of tips.

The money allowed me to buy the very first television my family ever had. The store I bought it from trusted me and let me buy it on credit for $25, when I was nine years old. The television was a floor model with a 12 inch screen. We watched lots of children's programs on that television. It worked well for many years.

My father wrote a letter to my sister Trudy, three months before he died, in which he wrote, "Bobby is still selling papers he is some boy believe me". My family always referred to me as Bobby.

I purchased a new bike when I was ten years old using the layaway plan from a Montgomery Ward store. A few weeks later it was run over by an eighteen wheel truck, which was backing up in a driveway where I had parked my bike while selling papers. The truck company paid for the bike and I put that money in my savings account. One great experience that came out of my elementary school experience was learning to save and manage money. The school required every student to open a savings account at a local bank. I made regular deposits with my earnings.

After that, I decided to buy a large upright piano. I paid $15 for it, which was a lot of money in those days. When they delivered the piano, it would not fit in the door of our apartment on School Street. I told them to put it in the alleyway adjoining our apartment building. When I bought the piano, it was summertime. As winter approached, I would visit my snow covered piano in the alley. I would brush off all the snow. The piano eventually rotted from the bad weather, fell apart and became part of the debris when the apartment complex was demolished the next year.

We were only paying $5.50 a week in rent for that three-story apartment, which was scheduled for demolition. I shared a bed in a very small room with four of my siblings: Shirley, Danny, Nancy, and Larry. There were five of us in one double size bed. Three of us slept at the head of the bed and two slept at the bottom. Peeling plaster fell from the walls in the apartment which was infested with rats and roaches.

The rooms on the second floor where my parent's bed and our bed were located were heated with a wood stove. I used to worry that the stove would catch the house on fire. I often stayed awake to monitor the stove as it became hotter and turned bright red. In the cold winters of New Hampshire, ice would form on the inside of the window just a foot from the head of our bed. We only had one blanket and shivered from the cold when trying to sleep. Sometimes, our older siblings threw their jackets over us when they returned home, which helped us stay warm on very cold nights.

There was no door between our bedroom and my parent's bedroom. I could easily see their bed from our bed. On several occasions, when my mother was sleeping alone, I would wake up and find her convulsing in an epileptic seizure. When that happened, I would jump out of bed, straddle her and pull her arms away from her throat as she seemed to want to strangle herself. My older siblings shared bedrooms on the third floor.

Our apartment was in a long row of apartments close to the factories. One of our neighbors was a family that would eventually include 24 members. They were called "the buggies" because the children were constantly sent home with lice. The family became a household name in our city because of their reputation for living in filth and destroying any apartment or house they rented. When a neighborhood learned they were going to move into their area, they hired lawyers to stop them. Because we were neighbors for a few years, we became friends with the family. Years later, I decided to study their family history with the community, city, and state and published the results in my Master's degree thesis.

We were living in this apartment at 23 School Street in Nashua when my father passed away. Our mother was left to care for the nine children still living at home. (As mentioned earlier, Trudy and Charlie had joined the Air Force.) My mother would outlive my father by fifty years, mainly by maintaining healthy eating habits. She boiled all her food, and avoided fatty foods, back in the 1960's when that was not necessarily the trend in cooking. She also stayed active, sociable, and never hesitated to see a doctor when she was not feeling well.

Soon after the funeral, my mother found another apartment close to downtown Nashua. She warned us not to tell anyone for fear that the owner of the apartment complex would change his mind about renting to our large poor family. After we moved, my sister Nancy's behavior became more aggressive. She would open other people's mailboxes and remove their mail. She also broke windows when she became angry. In 1956, when Nancy was eight years old, my mother requested that the state take over her guardianship. Nancy was placed at Laconia State School for the Feeble Minded, which had been established by the state for the mentally ill. It should have never been called a school as there was never any effort to educate or rehabilitate the residents.

Laconia State School for the Feeble Minded was a warehouse for those who were mentally disturbed and whose families did not want them or who were unable to care for them. The living conditions were once compared to concentration camps in Europe. There was one toilet for 80 residents, and that toilet did not even have a toilet seat. In 1991, it was shut down and the remaining residents were sent to foster homes or group homes. I did not become aware of the history and the conditions at the school until Nancy was sent to another home in 1982. When we had visited her in Laconia, we were only allowed to visit in a visiting room. We were never allowed to visit her residence so were not aware of the conditions at the school. I have and will always have a special, very loving, relationship with Nancy.

My oldest brother Buddy took over as the head of the household when my father passed away. He took his responsibility seriously and helped my mother meet the needs of housing and feeding our large family. He was often beaten by my father as a child and it was the only form of discipline he had learned growing up. He was ruthless when it came to punishing any of us for violating any of his many autocratic rules. He used his fists to hit us on the head and body. If we made any noise after being ordered to bed, he would come into the room and beat all of us with his fists and a large wooden board.

One day, when I was about 13 years old, I was a few minutes late arriving for dinner. As I arrived at the top of the stairs, he jumped out of his chair, knocked me to the floor, and straddled me, pinning me to the floor with his bodyweight. In front of the rest of the family he pushed my face into the floor, and sitting on my back, he punched me with both fists continually in the head. It was a brutal beating by a family member that I would never forget.

The anger and unhappiness of those around me while I was growing up caused me to exhibit unusual behaviors at thirteen years of age. I recall coming out of a shower that had been constructed in a closet that opened into our living room in our apartment. My brothers began bullying me, so I took my towel and threw it at them and then ran out into the back yard naked. The ground was covered with a foot of snow and it was snowing heavily. I ran down a flight of stairs and around the yard, naked and yelling as a reaction to the bullying. I was bullied at school and at home. My mother and family members were shocked at my behavior and thought I was seriously disturbed.

A few months later, for a reason unknown to me, I was sent to a medical doctor. My family was told that I had an irregular heartbeat. When I returned home, everyone treated me like I was going to die soon. Evidently, there was some confusion as to the condition of my health. The sympathy did not last long and everything returned to normal soon after. Our family was eventually asked to leave the apartment complex because of the behavior of my siblings and we moved to a duplex on Otterson Street, close to the City Hall.

I entered the 6th grade while living on Otterson Street. In the 6th grade, I had a teacher, Ms. McDonald, who was not as kind or understanding as Ms. Theros. In her classroom, I had my first panic attack as a result of being claustrophobic. The episodes became increasingly worse, to the point where I did not want to go to school. School's Staff told my mother I had developed school phobia. It was the most difficult year of my early education. I was forced to return to school and struggled with the panic attacks. They often distracted me from learning, but I learned to partially manage them.

The following year, I entered Nashua Junior High School as a 7th grader. I was bullied and harassed in junior high. Teachers ignored my needs. When I raised my hand to ask a question, a teacher (and also the school counselor), Ms. Winn, told me to put my hand down as I would never finish school. She said I had no right to ask questions. Ms. Winn chastised me every time she gave me a lunch card that allowed me to eat free. She made me feel worthless.

While I was a student in the 7th grade, my brother Pat robbed a store with an accomplice and in the process locked the employee in a large freezer located in the store. They were quickly apprehended and a front page story was written about the robbery, and what was considered an attempt to murder the employee during the robbery. A brother of the victim happened to sit next to me in one of my classes. It was tough going to school the morning the newspaper article appeared, as I knew I would have to sit next to a student whose brother had been assaulted and robbed by my brother.

On the playground during the lunch period, students would chase after me and play a game where I was considered the germ. They would laugh and yell, "Don't touch the germ" and then run away, after I chased after them, in fear of being touched. They did this because I wore dirty and smelly clothes. The harassment taught me to pay more attention to my personal appearance. I began to buy my own clothes and do a better job of maintaining my personal hygiene. I was still selling newspapers and I then added a new job, babysitting, to increase my income as a thirteen year old.

I did babysitting for my sister Marti and also my brother Fred. Marti was married and had two children at the time. She lived in the same apartment complex as my brother Fred on Vine Street. Sometimes, I spent the night at my sister's house. She was very nurturing and cared about her siblings more than any other sibling in my family.

As a thirteen year old, I was familiar with sex as I had often observed my brothers or visitors engage in sex in our apartment, which had no bedroom doors. However, no one had really discussed sex with me until one day my sister Marti asked me if I had ever had sex. After responding in the negative, she told me that her friend, a married woman in her early 20's with two children, was coming over after school the next day and she wanted to meet me.

I went over there after school and found her friend wearing a very sexy transparent nightgown. She had large breasts, a slim waist and looked very beautiful in her see-through nightgown. It was obvious that she was planning to have sex with me. I just pulled my pants down to my knees and it was all over in a few minutes. I lost my virginity at thirteen, with a married woman and mother of two. I had always been told by family members that sex was the greatest experience in life. When I left the apartment, I was disappointed. I was told by my three brothers, who had sex with her, that she was a nymphomaniac. I realized later that what happened with the nymphomaniac was not the same sex that people in love share.

We moved several times during my early teen years. We were on welfare by the time we moved to Otterson Street. We were often visited by social workers. My two older brothers, Charles and Pat, and one of their friends, John, (who was dating my mother) were all unemployed and were living with us. My mother was told by the welfare office that they would cut her welfare payments if she did not remove the older siblings and their friend from the apartment. They decided to sleep in a car parked in the driveway.

I remember going to school when there was three feet of snow on the ground and seeing the three of them fully clothed and asleep in the non-operational car covered with snow. We had to move out of this duplex apartment because of a fire in our apartment. After the newspaper reported that our large single parent family was displaced due to fire, we received some donations, and an apartment above an abandoned bakery that was located for us on West Pearl Street.

In 1958, my mother was becoming very frustrated at trying to care for the four children still living at home, and her older siblings who would move in with us whenever they were out of work. After she had Nancy placed at Laconia State School in 1956, she started to consider placement of the four younger children (Shirley, Robert, Danny and Larry), in foster homes. In November 1958, a director of welfare programs in Nashua wrote a letter to my sister Trudy, who was living in California, and informed her of my mother's plans to place the children in foster homes. Trudy was asked if she was willing to care for "Robert 13, in the 8th grade" or any of the other brothers

17

and sisters. In the letter, the agency reports, "We have recently had Robert tested by a psychologist who found him of average intelligence with possibilities of functioning within the bright normal range of intelligence". Since I did not move to California until May 1961 on my own accord, the answer must have been in the negative. Soon after that, my mother met her future husband, so the decision to place any of the five younger children into foster homes was placed on hold.

My older brothers often moved in with us as they had no other place to live. The apartment on West Pearl Street had only two bedrooms, with no doors and one bathroom, which our large family had to share with a man who lived in an adjoining apartment. Oftentimes, when all the siblings and their friends stayed overnight, my brother Danny and I had to sleep in the closet on top of a large pile of dirty laundry.

My mother became friends with the man next door, Leon Cassavaugh, and married him on August 22, 1959. He was in his 50's and had never been married. He immediately made every effort to evict my brothers and sisters from our apartment. The older brothers did not like him and quickly moved out. He eventually convinced my mother to send all my younger brothers and an older sister to foster homes, except me. I successfully resisted going to a foster home. Buddy married and moved out soon after his wedding.

Around this time, I was conducting research on military academies for middle and high school students. I was fascinated with the military and felt it was my calling. After I learned of the many military academies, I sent for and completed applications. They all required a large deposit to register for admission, which I could not afford.

In the 1950's there was a television series called, West Point. It involved life at the United States Military Academy at West Point and various situations involving Cadets. I was determined to attend West Point. When I went to the library my interest was totally focused on books related to military strategy and battles. However, my interest in the military and all my applications to private military academies did not change the fact that social agencies were planning to send me to a foster home.

I did not want to go to a foster home and had plans to live on my own after my 16th birthday in December 1960. I had saved a large sum of money from my newspaper route, my babysitting, working as a dishwasher in a restaurant, and from delivering Western Union telegrams. Before I turned 16 I had decided not to return to school, where I felt I was discriminated against. I had received almost all failing grades on my report card. I did not feel I was learning anything at that school and dropped out in the middle of the 10th grade. I also knew that having to work to live on my own would not allow me the time to continue in school.

A few days after my 16th birthday in December 1960, I packed a few clothes and asked my sister Marti for a ride to Manchester where I intended to find a job and live on my own. Manchester is the largest city in New Hampshire. The city had several factories where I believed I could obtain a full-time job. I quickly found a room to rent in a large building, for $15 a week, and a menial job in a shoe factory. The job was forty hours a week and paid $1.00 an hour. My job was to rotate shoe racks to about 15 women, who would pack the shoes in boxes.

The employees, mostly women twice my age, were kind, nurturing and often discussed their families with me. I learned several lessons as a 16-year-old at that factory. One day I learned an important lesson from a foreman on the ethics of working that would help me succeed later in life. He approached me on a day when there was not too much work to complete. He asked me what I was doing. I told him nothing. In a very stern voice, he told me never to say I was doing nothing. I was always to respond that I was looking for something to do. After that lesson on work ethics, I learned to always look for something to do, whenever I was working.

Another lesson I learned from that shoe factory was to never enter into a business relationship without documentation. A fellow employee asked me to invest a week's salary in a large boat that he was restoring. He explained in great detail all the work he was doing. I invested in the boat. However, I never saw the boat, nor received documentation of my alleged half ownership and ended up losing all of my investment. The lesson taught me to always demand documentation and seek detailed information on future investments.

Within a week of moving to Manchester, two policemen knocked on the door to my room in the rooming house and questioned me about my situation. I explained that I had my own apartment, a job, my parents' permission, and that I was qualified to be emancipated. My days in the library had helped me learn the rules regarding emancipation and the laws that govern children. They did not accept my explanation and requested that I call my mother on a pay phone. She told the police officer that I had her permission to live on my own. The police never questioned me again about my status. I will always appreciate my mother for supporting my move out of our home at age 16. She could easily have denied her permission and I would have been forced to move to a foster home or return to her home, where I was not wanted.

I did not like my new, but Spartan one room rental with no kitchen or living room. On the day I moved into the apartment, the manager observed me moving. When she saw me carrying an iron, she told me it was not allowed. Within a few weeks, I moved to a furnished apartment at 22 Concord Street. It had a separate bedroom, living room and kitchen, for a few dollars more. This manager, a very elderly gentleman, was very considerate. On the day I moved out of that apartment, he met me at the front door at 4:00 am to bid me farewell.

Soon after arriving in Manchester, I paid $50 cash for a blue, 1951 Plymouth four-door sedan. I was able to talk a co-worker into providing me with driving lessons so that I could obtain a driver's license. On the Sunday he was scheduled to give me a lesson, he did not show up. I decided, with no driving experience, to drive the car out on the streets. As I was turning a corner, I hit another car.

The driver, an elderly gentleman, was obviously angry at seeing a boy driving a car, who did not have the experience to merely turn a corner. Fear raced through my body. I have always had a fear of being arrested and placed in jail because of my claustrophobia and my family's history with the police. I gave the elderly driver my name and address and ran away from the scene. I ran to an office building in downtown Manchester and knocked on several doors, hoping to find a lawyer to help me.

Since it was a Sunday, I had to knock on many doors before I found a lawyer working in his office. He listened to my story and together we went to the police station to report the accident. I was given two tickets: one for failing to keep to the right of the road, and one for driving without a license. The police released me and gave me a date to report to court. A few weeks later, two policemen knocked on my door and demanded the license plates to my car. My car, just like my piano, ended up being useless to me.

I registered at a school that gave driving lessons and eventually learned to drive. I did not apply for a driver's license in New Hampshire because I was preparing to move to New York City. I was planning to leave in time to attend the graduation ceremony at West Point. I was obsessed with military history and the idea of graduating from West Point. I had decided I wanted to attend West Point early in my life. However, dropping out of high school in 1960 appeared to end that dream. I felt that even if I could not be a West Point cadet, I could go visit and attend the graduation. I wrote to my sister in California in April 1961 of my plans to move to New York in May.

My sister, Trudy, wrote me and told me if I could travel from New Hampshire to Lompoc, California, at my own expense, I could live with her and her family. One day I read an advertisement in the paper listed by a man who wanted someone to share expenses to Arizona. I figured Arizona was close to California, so I arranged to go with him. I quit my job, packed one suitcase, and left for California in early May 1961. I gave my car to my brother Danny who was living in a foster home at the time.

The trip to Arizona was uneventful. I remember the gentleman telling me that I looked like the new President, John Kennedy. In Arizona, we parted ways. I gave a lot of thought about how I needed to change my life. It was very hot in Arizona and I had never experienced such hot dry weather. As I reflected on my new situation, I decided to throw my black leather jacket decorated with chains into a trash can. To me, it was symbolic of changing my life. The leather jacket was left over from my days as a member of a teenage gang back in Nashua. I wanted to end that part of my life and attempt to forget the many bad memories of growing up in a dysfunctional poor family.

From Arizona, I took a train to Los Angeles. I had no map, but somehow managed to figure out I needed to get to Los Angeles. When I arrived I made my way to a bus station from the train station. In the bus station, I was approached by people who wanted me to go with them. I had no idea what they wanted. As a sixteen-year-old boy in a strange place, it was scary! All I wanted was to get on that bus to Santa Maria, California, which was close to Lompoc. My sister Trudy, her husband Ralph, and their two children, Mike (7) and Terrie (5), met me at the bus station. My reception was cold; I immediately felt unwelcome. My sister, who was eight months pregnant, never thought I could travel to California on my own. She later admitted that at 28 years old, she had neither the skills, nor the desire to care for a teenage brother because of her growing family's needs.

My brother-in-law was in the Air Force. He was preparing to retire with the rank of captain, and had already obtained a job with the General Electric Company. When I arrived, they were living on Vandenberg Air Force Base but were in the process of moving to a house they had purchased in Lompoc. My sister resented my presence in her home. I reminded her of our dysfunctional family and her earlier life living in poverty and she became very distressed over it.

At the time, I didn't understand why she was always angry with me. On at least one occasion, she slapped me across the face. However, I felt it was because I did not have the social graces that one demonstrates as a member of the middle class, as she had now become. In 2009, she wrote to me and explained her reasons, "There were so many priorities to worry about without having to take on the problems of my sixteen-year-old brother. I thought I could do it but I just wasn't prepared for what was facing me at that naïve and inexperienced age of 28".

I was an under-educated, lower class, and immature boy, lacking basic social graces. My brother-in-law tried to help me with some social manners. He told me that when I meet someone, I should ask them, "How are you?" I told him that I thought that was stupid. I asked him why I should care how they are. One day, my sister, told me to close the door when I came into her new house, and added, "Do you live in a barn?" I replied, "Yes". I was rude, immature and so very weak with interpersonal relations.

My sister demanded that I had to find a job to earn money and help pay expenses. I loved to work so I did not think that was going to be a problem. I quickly found a manual labor job with a tile installer. I helped him pull up old tile and install new tile in cafeterias on the Air Force Base. However, in order to report for work, I had to walk a half mile in the dark to the highway, and hitchhike a ride to the Air Force base, 12 miles from my sister's home. There were no street lights on the highway and the drivers that passed me had a difficult time seeing my arm stretched out and my thumb raised up begging for a ride. It was scary and dangerous.

A few weeks after my arrival, my sister told her husband she wanted me out of the house. On June 9, 1961, I returned late from work because I had to walk a long way from where I was dropped off. It was very dark and I recall wetting my pants while taking the very long walk to my sister's house from the highway.

When I entered the house, I quickly went to the bedroom to change. Before I could change, Ralph came up behind me and told me that my sister was in the hospital to have the baby and she wanted me to move out before she returned home. I told him that was no problem, and that I would leave immediately. He said I didn't have to leave immediately, but I didn't want to stay where I wasn't wanted. I had left my family home in New Hampshire for the same reason.

I packed my suitcase and went out to the dark highway and hitchhiked to Santa Maria which was about 25 miles away. I read an advertisement placed by an elderly lady who had a room for rent and I moved in with her. However, I was afraid and lay in bed at night, thinking she was going to kill me in my sleep. Obviously, I had seen too many horror movies. Around 2:00 am, I got out of bed, grabbed my suitcase and left her house. As I was leaving, she yelled out to me, "It's okay, you will be alright here". I went to the bus station and that is where I spent the rest of the night. In the morning, I went to see my sister, who happened to be in the hospital in Santa Maria, to check on her well-being. I lived on the streets for several days. I finally went to a social agency for assistance, as I had no idea what else to do. I had never imagined I would be kicked out of my sister's house, over 3,000 miles from my home in New Hampshire, after only a few weeks.

The California social agency contacted social agencies in Nashua, and obtained information on me. Unknown to me, social workers visited my sister in her house and made a deal with her. They wanted her to pay for my fare back to New Hampshire or consider allowing me to stay with her until I was old enough to join the Army at seventeen, which was six months away. She did not want to pay the fare, so agreed to let me return to the house. I was never told about the arrangement until the middle of December, just before I turned 17.

I returned to my sister's house in Lompoc, my job with the tile installer, and hitchhiking. Every morning, I walked up to the highway at 5:00 am, and in total darkness, attempted to hitch a ride to work. It was scary; I was only 16 years old. I worried about getting hit by a car because cars and trucks drove at 60 miles an hour past me and it was still so dark at that time of the morning. While waiting for a ride, I often wondered what kind of people demand that a 16-year-old stand on a dark highway at 5:00 am to hitchhike to work and then back home after dark. I began to resent my sister for kicking me out of the house after only a few weeks and requiring me to wait on that dark, lonely and dangerous highway for a ride to work.

Ralph often talked to me and gave me advice on many subjects. He was only forty years old when he retired from the Air Force. His plan was to work for General Electric and then retire from that company in twenty years, when he would be 60. He told me he wanted to have a comfortable retirement and planned on collecting three retirement checks when he was 62: one from the Air Force, one from General Electric and one from Social Security.

I remembered that advice in my own life because I also wanted a comfortable retirement in the future. Ralph was one of the kindest, most considerate men I have ever met and my life was better and more successful because of knowing him. Trudy divorced him a few years after I joined the Army and she would later tell me that divorcing him was one of the worst decisions she ever made.

In late summer of 1961, I applied and was accepted to serve as a counselor for a three-week camp for children on the base. It was a welcome relief from the tiling job and having to hitchhike to work every day. Since I had regular hours, Ralph gave me a ride to work and back to the house each day. One of the most enlightening experiences I had as a 16-year-old boy was when the young children I was supervising helped me become aware of a childhood experience that revealed my prejudice.

One day, I had about 10 children sitting on the ground and we had to select someone to be "it" for a game. I began to recite the rhyme I had been taught when I was young child. All the children became alarmed when I arrived at the word "nigger" in the rhyme—and so did I. I quickly learned from children under 10 years old that "nigger" was a very bad word. The rhyme I quoted was:

> Eeny, meeny, miny, moe,
> Catch the nigger by the toe.
> If it hollers/screams let him go,
> Eeny, meeny, miny, moe, you are it!

The response of the very young children stunned me and I would soon begin a lifetime commitment to improving race relations.

In September, my sister had to allow me to register for school because California had a compulsory education law. I was excited to be in school with children my own age. It was a lot different than working at hard labor all day with a sixty-year old man. I was very surprised at how much I enjoyed school. The enjoyment partially came from receiving "A" and "B" grades, rather than all the "F" grades I had received in my high school in Nashua.

The teachers were supportive and took the time to help me with all my courses. I had homework and completed it at home. For the first time in my life, I began to feel happy and content with my life. That happiness would soon end with a major surprise that resulted in a turning point in my life: my sister ordered me to quit school and join the Army.

My sister, unknown to me until later in life, had become very angry because she found out that I had discussed my poor environment and my family situation in New Hampshire. She had deliberately kept her upbringing secret and felt I was a threat to her image in the community as a member of the middle class. In December 1961, I learned about the deal made between the social agency and my sister in the summer. I was told to enlist in the Army on my 17th birthday, which would relieve both the social agency and my sister of my care and responsibility.

I recall going to all my teachers with my withdrawal papers. My teachers asked me why I was quitting and I could not keep back my tears. I wanted to graduate from high school in Lompoc, California and was very unhappy that I was being forced to quit. The Army had arranged for me to take a bus to Los Angeles to take a physical and be inducted into the Army on December 29, 1961. On the day I entered the Army, according to the Army; I was 5'8" and weighed 124 pounds. I was often told that I appeared to be too young to be in the Army.

The doctor who examined me said he could not approve my physical examination because I had a rash and I would have to return in a few weeks. I told him that I had no place to go and begged him to approve my physical, which he did. When the Army learned that I was only 17, an official told me that I could not be inducted without my mother's permission. The Army called my mother and once again she gave me the freedom to move on with my life. During my brief stay with my sister in California, I had read about the war in Vietnam and told her I wanted to go there. She thought it was a ridiculous idea and told me to stop thinking about it, and until 1968, I did.

Nashua, NH, 1949. Left to right: Danny (3), Author (4) and Shirley (5).

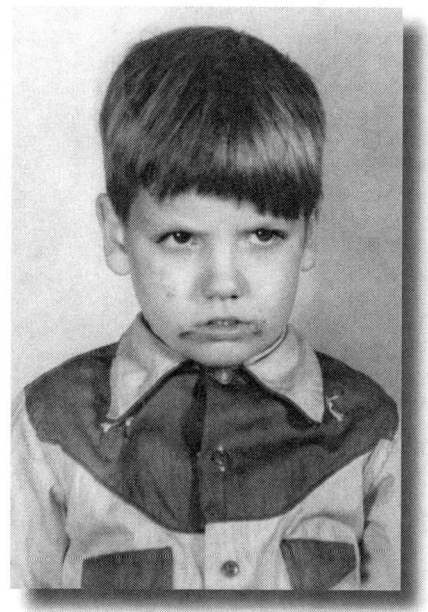

Nashua, NH, 1950. Author (6).

Nashua, NH, 1952. Author's parents: Leslie and Nancy Kimball.

Nashua, NH, 1954. Left to right: Charles Kimball (18), US Air Force,
and Leslie Kimball (64).

Nashua, NH, 1958. Author (14).

CHAPTER TWO

Beginning the journey to become an Army Officer
(1961–1968)

When I learned that I would be forced to join the Army in December of 1961, I visited a neighbor who was a retired World War II veteran, Colonel Harris, for advice. I told him I wanted to select the Infantry as my field of choice when entering the Army. When I had studied military history as a teenager, I was always impressed with the soldiers who fought directly with the enemy on the front lines. He advised me against going into the Infantry. He advised me to learn how the Army operates by selecting the Personnel Administration specialty field. After gaining that experience, if I still wanted to go into the Infantry, I could do so. It was excellent advice and I followed it. I learned how the Army operated administratively, how to type, and I attended classes in English grammar. I quickly became aware in these classes how poor my writing skills were, so I enrolled in English correspondence courses. Those correspondence courses prepared me for college courses I would enroll in within a few years.

Fort Ord, California, was a sprawling Army base close to the city of Monterey, where new recruits were trained. When I arrived on December 30, 1961, the base was celebrating the Christmas holidays. I spent the first fourteen days restricted to barracks, awaiting the beginning of my nine weeks of basic training. It was a lonely time, with no family or friends around during the holiday season.

The Army required new recruits to take many tests prior to beginning training. There were about 400 of us in the testing hall. At the time, I had no idea what the tests were all about. Later, I learned that one of them was a General Educational Development Test (GED), which is for a high school equivalency credential. I passed that test and was pleasantly surprised when I received a certificate of high school equivalency in January 1962.

Because I scored well on what was considered an IQ test, the GT test, I was given a test to determine if I qualified for the Officer Candidate School (OCS). Of the 400 recruits in the testing hall, only 75 were selected to take the OCS test. I was told I had the third highest score. All of this came as quite a surprise to me, since I felt that my poor background in education would keep me from being successful in life.

While waiting for basic training to begin, I was assigned to Kitchen Police (better known as KP duty). This duty consisted of spending long hours cleaning the kitchens of the mess hall where soldiers ate their meals. The Kitchen Police were given the most distasteful jobs in the kitchen such as cleaning grease traps. We had to work 12-14 hours a day and when we were finished, our bodies and uniforms were filthy.

Even after basic training began, which involved a seven-day work week, I was often assigned to KP duty by the drill sergeants. I felt they were harassing me because I had difficulty staying in step when marching and keeping up with other recruits during physical training. I decided to go to the Fort Ord Base Inspector General (IG) to complain about being given KP duty almost every day. Every military base has an Inspector General whose job it is to investigate complaints. The duty of kitchen police was supposed to be rotated fairly among all recruits. I also complained that I was charged with leave (vacation time) during the Christmas holidays while I was restricted to the barracks.

I appeared at the IG office wearing my dirty uniform after being on KP duty for 12 hours. The IG office called the commander and reprimanded him for having a soldier looking the way I did and ordered him to cease putting me on KP duty every day. After the phone call, I was able to join in the training with everyone else and given back my leave time. My salary as an Army private was a total of $78 a month, before taxes, which amounted to about 20 cents an hour (when you look at a 30 day month and 12 hour work days).

Drill sergeants in 1962 were World War II and Korean War veterans. They knew from battle experiences what we had to learn to survive war. They had no qualms about abusing us mentally and physically. To them, I was a small boy who should not be in the Army. The drill sergeants singled me out for harsh treatment because they probably felt I would never survive combat or I would get others killed in battle. I think they were hoping I would request an early discharge from the Army. I had difficulty keeping up with most of the training activities because of my small size and lack of agility. I was not used to shaving every morning and felt I did not need to, because there was almost nothing to shave. However, my drill sergeant thought differently. He reprimanded me and threatened me with a court martial if I failed to shave every day. Perhaps this is why, even in retirement, I shave every day, 7 days a week, 365 days a year.

The barracks was a two story building. There were about 40 bunk beds on each floor and 20 bunk beds on each side of the room. At the end of each bunk we placed a footlocker for storage of our clothing and toilet articles. The bathroom consisted of about eight commodes, all in a row, with no walls for privacy, some urinals, and about fifteen sinks. The lack of privacy in the restroom was difficult for me to adjust to. About two weeks into my training, I was dragged into that restroom by 30 members of my platoon for a "Code Red".

The drill sergeant in charge of our platoon was especially harsh to me. He would tell everyone in the platoon that I could not march and that the entire platoon was a disgrace because of me. He decided that I should get a Code Red. This is where members of your organization overwhelm you, force you naked into a shower and inflict bodily harm. Two soldiers who were in my platoon warned me about the Code Red. The night it was supposed to happen, I placed one combat boot on each side of my bottom bunk to use for defense. I had no fear and was prepared to fight them all, for daring to inflict bodily harm on me. Around midnight, I heard the feet of many soldiers coming down the stairs. Then everyone on my floor started rising from their bunks, to join in on the Code Red.

When they approached me, I jumped out of my bed swinging with a combat boot in each hand. The two soldiers who had warned me came to my defense but were quickly subdued. One received a bloody noise in the altercation. I was attacked by about 30 men, who tried to rip my clothes off and inflict bodily harm. I moved very quickly to push them away and struck many of the men while swinging my boots at them.

As we approached the door to the bathroom, I placed both of my feet on the door frame and pushed back, causing many of my assailants to fall down. They recovered quickly and were able to get me into the bathroom. However, before they could strip me and push me into the shower, the duty sergeant showed up and stopped the Code Red. Because I had kept my body moving and my boots swinging, no one had been able to land a punch on me, and fortunately, I came out of the experience without a scratch.

The next morning, as was his custom, our platoon sergeant came into the barracks to inspect us as we stood by our bunks. When he arrived in front of me, he brought up the weather. It was snowing, which was rare in this coastal area of California. He asked me if I had ordered it from my home state of New Hampshire. He then asked me how my night was. I told him it was wonderful and that I had slept well. After that incident, I was never harassed by my fellow recruits or drill sergeants.

A few weeks later, we were all given permission and the privilege of going to the Post Exchange, an Army shopping area. My fellow recruits who had participated in the Code Red acted like they were my best buddies and comrades. They introduced me to drinking beer at the age of 17, with the goal of helping me become intoxicated.

They succeeded. I returned to the barracks that night totally intoxicated. I then tried to escape through a window to get more beer. Fortunately, my fellow recruits physically restrained me from leaving the barracks until I passed out. The military training I received in the Army from 1961-1964 would help me survive the Vietnam War (1968-1969, 1970-1971) and become an Army leader.

As I write this, I am reminded of a story I read in the paper recently (March 2011) of how the Army is changing basic training because soldiers in Iraq and Afghanistan were not physically prepared for battle. One general complained that very few soldiers and marines have ever been slapped or punched in the face. He felt that soldiers were shocked when they encountered a physical confrontation with the enemy. The new training program would include more physical interaction. I believe my training prepared me well for combat in Vietnam and I will always be appreciative of those combat veterans who trained me for war. Because of them, I was able to lead men in combat and help them and I survive war.

One of my training lessons involved being left alone, stuck on an obstacle course with no one to assist me. On a very cold rainy day, we had to go through an obstacle course that involved barbed wire and live fire. The exercise required us to lie on our backs, with rifle and helmet and then crawl under layers of barbed wire while live machine gun bullets were fired over us. The ground was wet and muddy and I got stuck half way. By the time it got dark, every other soldier had finished the drill and everyone was waiting on me to finish.

The senior drill sergeant, who always greeted us with a "fuck you" every morning when we said "good morning" to him, yelled a string of profanities at me and told me everyone was leaving the training area. That night, I was alone on that obstacle course, mired in mud, under the stars, with barbed wire covering my body. After an hour or so, I managed to get free by forcing my steel helmet into the mud and creating a crevice under the barbed wire for my body to move forward. Around midnight, someone came to check on me and returned me to the base.

During Army basic training I gained the courage to voice concerns to a higher authority when I was being treated unfairly.

The experience reinforced my belief that no one should accept harassment or unfair treatment. The Code Red taught me that not everyone will go along with a group consensus and there will always be someone that will do the right thing. I will always respect the two recruits who stood by me during that fight and tried to defend me.

The experience also reinforced what I had already come to understand: never fear in times of danger, and always be ready to challenge those who wrong you. The obstacle course taught me that sometimes you cannot depend on others to help you. Situations may develop where you are totally on your own and only you can resolve the situation. These experiences were immensely helpful as I pursued what would become a military career.

After basic training, I was assigned to Fort Benjamin Harrison, close to Indianapolis, Indiana, for six weeks of training in Personnel Administration. The Army arranged for me to ride a train to Indianapolis with other soldiers. The training turned out to be similar to attending college, in that we attended classes and there was no harassment or harsh treatment. I recall going to the club almost every night, drinking beer and listening to that depressing song, "Born to Lose", by Ray Charles.

The Army allowed 18-year-olds to drink on the base. I was only 17, but no one checked identification. While in Indianapolis, I had the opportunity to attend the Indy 500. Although sports in general, and motor racing in particular never interested me, I did have free tickets and it was an historical event, so I went along.

The six weeks went by quickly, and I received orders that assigned me back to Fort Ord as a Personnel Specialist.

At Fort Ord, I was responsible for maintaining the records of many soldiers. Reviewing those records was a learning experience for me. Most of the soldiers who had earned medals had detailed citations describing their bravery in battle in World War II or Korea, or both. However, I soon became bored with my job and wanted a change. At the Presidio of Monterey, a few miles from Fort Ord, there was an Army Language School that I wanted to attend. I submitted an application to my chain of command. I was informed that the only opening at the school was to study the Burmese language. I applied for that language, was accepted, and soon received orders to report in September 1962; I was only seventeen. Colonel Harris was right, learn the Army's system, and you can get just about anything you want.

The Burmese language course was scheduled for one year. Our class had a total of six students. One was a major, the most combat-oriented and impressive soldier I had ever met. He had a lot of experience all over the world as a Special Forces officer. Major Happerset was 40 years old and had a high school GED like myself. He introduced me to long-distance running.

We would meet nearly every week day and go for a five-mile run in the Pebble Beach area. He was in great physical condition but had a very difficult time learning Burmese. My other classmates were a black officer, an alcoholic sergeant (who did not finish the course), and two married soldiers who were about thirty years old.

Our daily schedule consisted of attending class from 8:00 am to 4:00 pm with one hour for lunch. We were required to study for three hours in the evening, memorize an assigned dialog, and be prepared to recite the dialog in the morning. We wore dress uniform to class. We had our weekends free. I didn't need to study at night as I had the ability to memorize the dialog in the twenty minutes before morning class began. The chairman of the Department admonished me for not studying more and I reminded him that I had an "A" average in the course. He never called me into his office again.

Our instructors were all born in Burma (now officially known as the Republic of the Union of Myanmar) and therefore were native speakers. I had the opportunity to get to know them on a personal basis. We went on several field trips and socialized frequently. We were never allowed to speak English in class. At the beginning of the course, as homework, we were told to cut out pictures that depicted Asian life and bring them to class. Rather than Asians, I cut out pictures of blacks in an African village and pinned them on the bulletin board. My homework definitely revealed my lack of knowledge of the world. After being embarrassed by my classmates, I was determined to learn more about world history and geography.

In my free time, I enjoyed reading the newspaper. One day I found an invitation to those interested in the U.S. Capitol to join an historical society. I sent in my $1 fee and received a letter from a U.S. Senator who informed me that I was the first to join the U.S. Capitol Historical Society from California. I also learned of an invitation for students to apply for a scholarship for a four-day World Affairs Conference that was going to be held in Monterey. I applied and received the scholarship and attended the conference in 1963.

Like most seventeen year olds, I wanted to own a car. I saved enough money to purchase a Mercury Monterey convertible that had leather seats and power windows. I bought the car from a dealership in Monterey for $268. It provided me with the freedom to leave the base and escort ladies on dates.

My first and only girlfriend in my first three-year tour in the Army was eighteen-year-old Josephina Gomez, who was working as a maid for a wealthy family. She was from Lima, Peru, and could speak no English. We communicated with a dictionary and body language. I often drove to Carmel Valley to visit her and I have fond memories of playing the radio very loudly and driving in my convertible with the top down, windows open, letting in the cool California air.

Josephina suddenly informed me she was pregnant and insisted that we marry immediately. At 18 years old, I was not ready for marriage. I also did not believe she was pregnant and suspected that she was just looking for a path to citizenship. She finally admitted she was not pregnant and concluded that she needed to find a man to marry so she could become a U.S. citizen. Josephina did find another soldier who would marry her.

My beautiful convertible needed repairs, which I could not afford. As a result, I had to give it up six months after purchasing it.

While at the Army Language School, I began to think about what I wanted to do after graduating. I had always wanted to be an officer, and had scored highly enough in testing to qualify, so I applied for OCS at Fort Benning, Georgia. As part of the application, I had to undergo a psychological evaluation by a psychiatrist. I knew that this would be a challenge with my dysfunctional poor background. I decided to go to the base library and conduct research on psychological evaluations. I found several examples and studied them in preparation for the evaluation.

During my evaluation, the doctor was suspicious and commented that I appeared to have studied the tests. However, he did approve my application. I was accepted to the Infantry Officer Basic Course (IOBC) at Fort Benning OCS and reported after my language course ended in September 1963. When I got off the bus, the bus driver warned me to look at the heading above the bathrooms. When I exited the bus, I could see that the bathrooms were labeled, "White Only" and "Negros". I quickly realized I was not in California or New Hampshire any longer.

When I arrived for infantry officer training, I was only 18 years old. All the other IOBC candidates were either college graduates or veterans who had been in the Army for between five and fifteen years. I was the only candidate under the age of 21. I was reminded daily that I looked younger than 18 years old. It seemed no one could understand why I was enrolled in the program except me.

During the IOBC, we were again subjected to physical and mental abuse. The person in charge of our platoon, referred to as a tactical officer, was a Lieutenant McConnell. He kept telling me I could not be the "boy wonder" because he was. He was married and was about 23 years old but looked very boyish. Upon meeting me, he informed me that I would never finish the program and he was personally going to have me kicked out as soon as possible because there could only be one boy wonder.

The purpose of the IOBC, which lasted for 24 weeks, was to prepare us to lead men in battle. The training was designed to change our behavior so that we would stay calm when everyone else was falling apart. One of the major objectives of the training was to teach the candidates to pay attention to detail, which is why the tactical officers were so demanding in their constant inspections. Training in the field forced us to function effectively, despite a lack of sleep and inadequate food. The goal was to make each of us technically and tactically proficient when leading soldiers.

Daily life at OCS involved going to sleep at around 2:00 am and waking up at 4:00 am to prepare for inspection. Each night we had to clean and shine our mud covered boots. Boots had to be shined to the point that you could see your reflection in them, and that task often took an hour or more. We also had to shine the linoleum floors so well that they, too, were bright and sparkling. When we were ready to sleep we could not step on the floor for fear of leaving a footprint. The tactical officers would assign demerits if they saw one footprint on the floor, which could even be caused by stepping on it in socks. Cleaning the bathrooms to their expectations took several hours every night.

The mornings began with an inspection by our tactical officer who would always assign me more demerits than anyone else. Demerits were assigned if he did not like the shine on your boots, found a shirt with a slight wrinkle or that was not hung up the way he wanted, discovered a hair on your face you missed while shaving, a buckle that was not shined well enough for him and anything else for which he could assign demerits. The demerits became a part of your training record. One day my tactical officer assigned me one demerit for each of 70 buttons I had not buttoned on shirts I had recently picked up at the cleaners.

After the inspection, it was time to move to the mess hall for breakfast. Several tactical officers were assigned to constantly harass us. While in line, you were told to do 50 push-ups for not looking straight ahead, for talking or for moving in any way the tactical officers did not like. The harassment was so intense at meal times that you rarely finished a meal.

The tactical officers would often have an officer candidate get on top of a table in the dining room and yell, "I eat like a pig, and I do not deserve to eat here". Lieutenant McConnell would take me to the kitchen and tell me in front of all the other candidates that I would be working in the kitchen soon because I was going to be kicked out of OCS. Candidates who were kicked out of the program were often assigned KP duty in order to humiliate them and set an example.

After a hurried, stressful breakfast; we would form up and prepare to go to the training scheduled for that day. There were six student leaders assigned to each five day period: a platoon leader, platoon sergeant, and four squad leaders. On one particular day, four tactical officers were yelling and screaming at all the student leaders. The purpose of this harassment was to place so much pressure on them that it would make us late for training and thus the student leaders would be written up for poor leadership.

On this occasion, I was not in a leadership position, but I decided to take control of a hectic situation. I stepped out of ranks, moved to the platoon leader's position in front of the 30-man platoon, and yelled, "Right face", followed by, "Forward March". The tactical officers were stunned and normally would have been happy to see someone take charge, but not me.

All four tactical officers, all lieutenants, began yelling and screaming at me for breaking ranks and challenging authority, but I ignored them and we marched off to training. Fortunately, the company commander, Captain Maggin witnessed my actions and commended me for taking the initiative to move the students to class when the other student officers were being harassed.

We attended classes on many subjects, including all types of weapons, tactical vehicles, map reading, hand-to-hand combat, and bayonet training. We often went to the range and fired almost every weapon in the Army's arsenal and we also went on many overnight trips to participate in war games. The training was tough, demanding and aimed at preparing us to stay calm and do well in battle as leaders.

While we were in the field on maneuvers in November 1963, we were ordered to return to our barracks on the base. We were then directed to form up outside the barracks. At a formation of all candidates, we were informed by our company commander that President John F. Kennedy and Vice President

Lyndon B. Johnson had been assassinated. Later, we were given an update that the Vice President had survived and was now our President. At the time, I had no emotional reaction to the news because my focus was on our leadership training. I also had very little knowledge of (or interest in) world events.

While our leadership training was going on, my tactical officer, to my disadvantage, often wrote me up for violating rules or failing to exhibit leadership traits. After twelve weeks of training, he recommended that I be dropped from the program. I had failed the map test which is a requirement for graduation and was one of the reasons he cited for removing me from the program.

At my hearing I fervently protested and begged to be allowed to complete the twenty-four week program. However, the members of the hearing board approved the recommendation for removal and accordingly my participation in the program was terminated. I was ordered to wait for my new assignment and was relocated to a nearby barracks. Because of my rank (Specialist E-4) I was not given KP duty, which was the usual way to humiliate privates, grade levels E-1, E-2 and E-3 who were removed from the program.

I decided to appeal the removal decision to the Deputy Commanding General of Fort Benning, Brigadier General Norton. General Norton was one of those few officers who became a general in World War II before he was 30 years old. I laid out my case to the general and he listened. His advice, recognizing that I was only 18, was to gain more experience and then return to officer school.

I was assigned to an administrative position on the base after being dropped out of the OCS course. On weekends, I traveled around the state by bus or hitchhiking. I learned more about race relations by witnessing segregation and racism while stationed in Georgia. The Governor of the State of Georgia at the time was a segregationist. Segregationists believed that Negros were an inferior race and insisted on enforcement of laws and traditions that required that they be legally separated from whites. They wanted to prevent Negros from sharing schools, restaurants, theaters, and transportation with whites, and prevent them from living in their neighborhoods. Negros who violated laws or traditions supporting segregation were often arrested, beaten and sent to jails.

The 1960's was a time of race riots, especially in the southern areas of the United States. Local racists were attacking and killing whites thought to be helping blacks. I constantly heard soldiers laughing at racists jokes, which dehumanized blacks. While stationed in Georgia in 1964, I learned that interracial couples were in violation of state law and would be arrested. The military did not assign mixed race couples to Georgia and other Southern states because of laws prohibiting interracial marriages. The Supreme Court of the United States ruled such laws unconstitutional in 1967.

I became keenly interested in racism and decided, as a strict opponent of racism, to attend a rally that supported segregation as a learning experience. White people who were opposed to segregation and showed up at the rallies were often beaten up; however, I decided to take a chance to attend so that I could learn more about hate. The Governor of Alabama, another segregationist, was one of the key speakers.

The rally was held at a football stadium and the stands were packed. When I tried to take pictures, I was given threatening looks by bystanders. I heard many speakers refer to blacks as being inferior and criticize the U.S. Government for taking up for blacks. It was an eye-opening experience and one that would motivate me to be a life-time advocate for the oppressed.

While waiting for my next assignment, I was housed in a barracks with forty bunk beds on both sides of a room three times larger than the room I lived in when attending basic training. My roommates often harassed black soldiers by running around the large room with sheets over their heads, acting like they were members of the Ku Klux Klan (KKK). I witnessed black soldiers with a look of fear on their faces that I would never witness again, except in battle. They also harassed some soldiers who were waiting to be discharged for homosexual activity. One of those soldiers changed my life by providing me advice and encouragement to obtain a higher education.

Robert Johnson and his twin brother, who were from Iowa, had almost completed officer training when Robert was kicked out for touching another male inappropriately. One day he invited me to a club for a beer. We met often and talked about everything except sex. For the first time, I learned about the existence of institutions of higher education. No one had ever discussed college with me; I had no idea what it was all about. He had graduated with a degree in education and talked to me about pursuing a degree. He suggested that I sign up for college English and History classes that were being offered by a university on the base.

I doubted I would do well since I had only completed the 9th grade and had mostly "F" grades on my report card. However, he made it clear that was what I had to do if I wanted to be an officer, so I registered for the courses. I was surprised when I earned "A" and "B" grades in some of the courses, and this helped motivate me to continue my education in college. After taking a few more courses, I was hooked, and had every intention of staying in college until I received a bachelor's degree.

While waiting for my three year tour of duty to end in December 1964, I learned that in the summer of 1964 my mother and aunt were going to visit my mother's family in Lexington, Virginia. I went to Lexington to meet them and filmed the visit with a wind-up 35 mm video camera. My grandfather was confined to a wheelchair and lived in a shack that lacked electricity and was missing some of its windows. I was fortunate to be able to take pictures of him and his three daughters together. I wrote of this experience in my first college English class. The professor was so impressed with my writing that he had me read it to the class. He told my classmates that I had a talent for writing, boosting my self-esteem.

When my three years of duty was up, I decided to leave the Army and attend college full time in California. I soon learned that the Army had another plan. The Army informed me that I had one more year to serve because I had signed an agreement to extend my service in return for accepting an assignment at the Army Language School. I began researching ways to get out of the one year extension on my contract. After reviewing

Army regulations, I found my way out. I had signed the contract as a seventeen-year-old. The Army requires parental approval for soldiers under eighteen to sign a contract. After I convinced the Army that they had made an error by not obtaining my mother's approval, I was released from my one year extension.

I was honorably discharged from the Army in December 1964. I informed my sister Trudy that I was returning to California to attend a junior college close to where her family lived. She advised me to not return to California but to stay in the Army. She made it clear in her letters that I would not receive any help from her. I informed her that I was not expecting help from her and would not ask for it.

I informed her I would be visiting our family in Nashua before traveling to California. In a letter on July 21, 1964, at the age of 31, Trudy wrote:

"Bobby when you go home you can tell Danny for me that if he continues to date that nigger. yes nigger. I've become very bitter! That I will completely forget I ever had a brother Danny—and when I do come home, perhaps next year, my children will not be introduced to him! And you know I mean it. What the h____is wrong with him! Is he illiterate—has he no pride. Can you imagine yourself being called Uncle by a black baby?? And you can tell him that it will be black! As you know the black genes dominate."

Many of my family members, even today, refer to blacks using the "N-word" in spite of having nieces, nephews and cousins who are black. I will always be thankful to the children who I supervised at a summer camp in 1961, for teaching me at the age of 16 that the N-word is a bad word and reflects poorly on one's attitude toward others.

After my discharge, I went to visit my family in Nashua. I filmed portions of the visit with my wind-up Browning 8 mm movie camera. While visiting, I decided to leave a locked footlocker full of mementoes with my mother, which my brother Danny later went through after cutting the lock. After a week with my family, I took a bus from Nashua to Santa Maria, California, to begin classes at Allan Hancock College in January 1965. I had no financial aid, nor family support to assist with my expenses.

I was not eligible for the G.I. Bill (originally the Servicemen's Readjustment Act of 1944, although the term has now come to include other veteran benefit programs) and had no idea how to obtain a loan. I had only my meager savings. I decided to join the California National Guard both to stay affiliated with the military and to generate an income.

I found an inexpensive room to rent near the college. My savings and income from the National Guard helped get me through my first semester. During the summer, I worked and saved money for the next semester. Prior to the fall semester, I searched for any available scholarships. I learned that I could apply for a $500 scholarship if I worked for the school newspaper. The only position open was as a sports editor. I knew very little about sports, but applied anyway, got the job and qualified for the scholarship.

This turned out to be a fortunate decision, because as sports editor, I was permitted to live on campus in the dormitory reserved for athletes. The monthly rental fee was only $10. I moved into a room that was small for two people, with a small sink and one window. There was one bathroom with showers shared by all the residents in the dormitory. Female guests were not allowed in the athlete's dormitory. However, I had female friends who would discretely come into the room through that one window.

Living with the athletes helped me get player interviews and then write my stories covering their games. They would explain the rules of football, baseball, and basketball so that I would sound more credible in my articles. I couldn't afford a meal card so I lived on cold canned food. My typical diet consisted of a piece of bread in the morning, a cold can of beans at lunch and a cold can of spaghetti for supper, and lots of water. There was no equipment to heat food in the room. I kept my food expenses under $1 a day.

As a member of the California National Guard, I attended one weekend drill each month. I applied, and was accepted to begin officer training at what the National Guard called the "California Military Academy". The training was held in Ventura, which was at least five hours drive from Santa Maria. I could not afford a car and taking the bus would have been too expensive and time consuming. Fortunately, another veteran, Robert Ulin, who lived close by and owned a car, had enrolled in the program. He picked me up and we took the five-hour drive together each weekend and summer.

In the summer of 1965, I found a part-time job working in a sign writing shop. In August, after a weekend at a secluded lakeside site, fishing with a co-worker and his family, I returned to my apartment, to find a notice on my door activating my National Guard unit for duty in response to the Watts Riots. In Los Angeles, black residents were gathering in the streets by the thousands to demonstrate against oppression and the denial of their civil rights. I reported to my unit and was driven to Los Angeles. We were not involved in any action; we just served as back-up forces to the police, if needed. Our unit was in Los Angeles for no more than ten days.

When I returned, I wrote a speech about how blacks were being oppressed and why blacks in Los Angeles were rioting. I spoke passionately about how nothing was being done to address their oppression. When community groups called my speech teacher requesting a speaker for their monthly meetings I was often recommended. I gave my speech on the Watts riots, without notes, to many community groups, who happened to be mostly white women in the Santa Maria area. They were quite surprised when I defended the rioters in Los Angeles. I told them that if I were black, I would have joined the riot. They reacted very politely and most likely concluded that I was a misguided young man.

I was short of funds for the fall semester and was concerned. As I searched for ways to finance my education, I learned that based on my father's work record, I was eligible for Social Security benefits until I was twenty-one years old. Those benefits, along with my National Guard drill pay, allowed me to continue my studies at Allan Hancock College.

I declared pre-law as my major, but when I realized I would not have enough funds to complete law school, I changed my major to social studies. I was granted 21 college credits with a grade of "A" for my studies at the Army Language School.

Those credits significantly improved my grade point average and helped me to qualify for admission to California Polytechnic State University (Cal Poly) in nearby San Luis Obispo.

In the summer of 1966, prior to beginning classes at Cal Poly, I was commissioned as an Army Second Lieutenant in the California National Guard, thereby achieving one of my goals of becoming an Army officer. I was assigned to be the leader of a National Guard Ordnance Unit in Atascadero, California. In order to get to the meetings, which were about twenty miles away, I had to walk to the highway and hitch a ride. I did not want to be in the Ordnance Corps and quickly had my assignment changed to a combat artillery unit. After receiving my commission, I found that I had enough funds to attend summer school at Cal Poly and registered for classes.

I looked in San Luis Obispo for a room to rent and decided on an inexpensive off-campus student complex that had a cafeteria. Each unit had three bedrooms, a large living room and could house five students. Tropicana Village had previously been open only to female students, whose parents wanted them to be supervised. However, management decided to open it up to men during the summer, minus the supervision. I was greeted at the reception desk by the assistant manager, Vyone Anderson, an attractive single blonde with blue eyes and a friendly smile. She had graduated from Cal Poly in 1965 and obtained the assistant manager position. Every day, I flirted with her, until finally I got her to agree to date me on a regular basis.

During the summer of 1966, I went on two, two-week National Guard summer camps to earn extra funds. My specialty area had been changed to Field Artillery. I was assigned as a fire direction officer to a field artillery battery. Our summer camp involved us travelling to the Mojave Desert and firing 155 mm towed howitzers. Performing the duties of fire direction officer required at least twelve weeks of full time training, which I had not yet received.

I had not been trained in the computations that determined what settings to give to the howitzer crews. Fortunately, others in the fire direction center did know how to do the computations. The battery commanding officer, a captain, then assigned me as a safety officer, which, again, demanded training and certification I had not received.

The captain immediately recognized that I was not trained in the duties of the fire direction officer or safety officer and concluded that I was not competent. The fact that I had not received the training did not seem relevant when he reported on my lack of abilities to his superiors and followed up with a very negative report on my performance. The captain decided to assign me additional duties, such as going back to the base and picking up truckloads of beer for the men.

When I returned to the camp site with the beer, I always tied empty beer cans on a long string of wire and dragged them behind the truck, so that the men could hear us coming from a mile away. On one of these trips across the Mojave Desert, I noticed a senior warrant officer carrying a woman in his arms across the open desert. They both appeared intoxicated.

I stopped to help him and he explained that he had picked up the much older woman, who had no legs, from a bar. Somebody had pulled a prank and taken her wheelchair from the bar. He said he needed to get back to the base but did not need a ride to our campsite. It was an eye opening experience and raised my tolerance level for being a witness to strange situations. After summer camp, I returned to my classes at Cal Poly. I had to move into the dormitory in the fall, because of the gender rules at the apartment complex. I continued dating Vyone, and always felt at ease and happy when I was with her. We had many mutual interests and were in agreement on most matters we discussed. I felt that it was the right time in my life to get married. I would soon obtain a college degree and had become an Army officer. I proposed marriage to her and she accepted. I had neither funds nor credit to buy fancy rings so I purchased a three ring set at a pawn shop for $34.00. She proudly showed off her engagement ring to everyone she knew. It had only a small diamond but it was a ring given to her by a man who loved her.

We could not afford a large wedding either, so we decided to get married in Solvang, California by a Justice of the Peace.

There were only a few guests at the wedding. My friend who motivated me to go to college, Robert Johnson, attended; along with my sister Trudy and her family. I wore a $13.00 suit I had purchased for the occasion and Vyone wore a blue suit that she had purchased for $35.00. After the wedding, we moved into a duplex apartment in Shell Beach, close to San Luis Obispo. I registered for classes in the spring of 1967 and was close to fulfilling the requirements for my Bachelor of Science degree.

Vyone became pregnant with our first child, due in June 1967. On the morning of June 20, 1967, I took her to the hospital and was told she may not deliver for several hours. I felt I had time to attend a review class for a final examination so went to the class. When I returned to the hospital, I was informed that she had delivered. I asked if it was a boy or girl. The Nurse yelled down the hall and asked that question, and the response was a boy. We named him James after Vyone's uncle, and gave him the middle name of Bradley after a famous World War II General.

In the early summer of 1967, my National Guard supervisors asked me to attend the Field Artillery Officer Basic Course at Fort Sill, Oklahoma in September that year. Since I had completed all my course work at Cal Poly and was only working on my thesis, which was required to graduate, I agreed to attend the Army's course. The training course was for twelve weeks. The training program was excellent and I learned how to perform the duties of a Field Artillery Officer.

One day while having dinner at the Officers' Club at Fort Sill, I was threatened by a black waiter. He asked me what the ribbons on my uniform were for. When I explained that one of them was for serving on active duty during the Watts riots, he became very irritated. Just prior to leaving, he whispered in my ear that if he ever saw me wearing that service ribbon outside of the club he would kill me. I understood his anger and never wore that service award again. My decision was not made out of fear, but out of respect for his feelings towards the oppression of blacks in the Watts neighborhood.

In 1968, the Army was recruiting National Guard officers to volunteer for active duty because the Vietnam War was in full swing. My goal had been to obtain a college degree and return to the Army as an officer. I submitted a request to return to the active Army. The Army had promised those who volunteered their choice of Army bases to be assigned to and I selected Fort Carson, Colorado. I received orders to report for duty in March 1968. Since I was not familiar with the housing or the work requirements, we decided that Vyone should remain in California until we decided it was time for her and our son to join me in Colorado. A few months later, I sent for my family and they joined me in Colorado Springs. The Army arranged for our household goods in San Luis Obispo to be sent to Fort Carson.

Fort Carson, just outside the city of Colorado Springs, was another sprawling Army base. The base was the home of the 5th Infantry Division of which I became a member. The unit I was assigned to be was Battery A, 6th Battalion, 20the Field Artillery. My position in the unit was battery fire direction officer, a job I had been trained for and was ready to perform. Our unit often went to the field to practice firing the 155 mm self-propelled howitzers.

In 1968, the Army, like many cities across the nation, had its troubles with race relations. Racial riots had been going on for several years and the Army was not exempt from the racial issues that were impacting many lives. When it was announced that Martin Luther King, Jr. had been assassinated on April 4, 1968, the Army anticipated a reaction from black soldiers and were prepared to be flexible.

The day after his assassination, black soldiers refused to form up with the other soldiers in the 6:00 am formation, called reveille. Military leaders made no effort to go into the barracks to find out what the black soldiers' plans were, but took a "wait and see" approach. After about an hour of waiting for a reaction, I witnessed an amazing and courageous reaction to the assassination from these black soldiers.

They came out of the barracks in a single file, not in uniform, and moved to the headquarters of the Battalion. They began walking in a circle around the battalion headquarters. The battalion commander and other leaders decided to allow the black soldiers to take the day off and demonstrate peacefully. I was proud of those black soldiers demonstrating courage by defying authority and expressing their anger at the state of race relations in America. The next day, the black soldiers returned to their routine, dressing in their uniforms and forming up in ranks, as was the custom in those days.

The Army is a very demanding social organization. Officers and their wives are required to attend many social functions. Some officers or their wives resented being forced to attend but we always felt it was a part of our job. At one of these functions, which was held outdoors, I wore bright orange trousers. The battalion commander said he never thought he would ever see one of his officers wearing orange pants and laughed about it.

The year was 1968 and when we did meet for social reasons in that year; all the talk was about the Vietnam War. I participated in some of these discussions and for the most part, the senior officers I met were opposed to the war. However, I wanted to experience war. When I was a teenager, I had told my sister that I wanted to go to Vietnam. The Army was asking for individuals who had not already been given orders for Vietnam, to volunteer to go. I submitted my application and was given orders to report to South Vietnam (officially known as the Republic of Vietnam) in September 1968.

I requested a thirty-day leave of absence before going to Vietnam. We decided to visit my grandfather in Lexington, Virginia, my family in New Hampshire and my friend Robert Johnson in Chicago. I had arranged for my mother to be in Lexington at the same time we were going to be there. On our first day in Lexington, we had a cordial visit with the family and took pictures of our son, with his grandmother and paternal great grandfather on the porch of the house. On the second day we were taken by surprise when the state police arrived to take my grandfather to the district home for the elderly and indigent in Waynesboro.

My grandfather was visibly upset and resisted the police, as he let out a string of profanities from his wheelchair. He refused to get into the police car and the situation became awkward as the three police officers tried to force a disabled

80-year-old man into their car. My aunts and mother asked my grandfather if he preferred to go in my car instead and he agreed. He calmed down and asked us to visit him again. After that depressing experience, we departed for New Hampshire. Unfortunately, I was not able to visit him again before he died on February 2, 1972.

In New Hampshire, Trudy and her children happened to be visiting at the same time. When we met her at Boston airport (now known as Boston Logan Airport), she was extremely emotional and upset, and she whispered in my ear that she had divorced Ralph, and didn't want the family to know. While in New Hampshire, I had my first opportunity to take a picture of my mother and all of her seven sons. After our visits to Virginia, New Hampshire, and Chicago, we returned to California so that Vyone and our son could move into an apartment close to her parent's house in Seaside, California, while I served in South Vietnam.

Army Language School, Monterey, CA, 1962. Author (17).

Seaside, CA, 1947. Vyone Kimball and her parents: Alvin and
Hannah Anderson.

Nashua, NH, 1968. Kimball family members: (from top row, left to right) Charles, Trudy, Mother, Patrick, Fred, Danny, Author and Larry.

CHAPTER THREE

Vietnam War Experiences
(1968-1969 and 1970-1971)

On the day that I began my journey to South Vietnam, my wife and son accompanied me to the train station in Monterey, California, to see me off to war. I was excited and looking forward to experiencing war. Vyone's father had served in World War II as a cook, and had participated in several campaigns, so she was aware of the sacrifices required of military families. I took the train to Tacoma, Washington, where I caught a civilian jet liner leased by the Army to ferry troops to Vietnam. Most of the soldiers in the jet were draftees, unwilling participants in this unpopular war. The flight lasted about 14 hours and was uneventful.

Replacements for the military in Vietnam were flown into Cam Ranh Bay and then out to their units. We were provided with comfortable beds, cafeterias, theaters, and bars; all of which were air-conditioned to make life comfortable. Living conditions were great and not at all what I had expected in a combat zone. Later I learned that of the 500,000 members of the military serving in Vietnam, only 10 percent were actually engaged in combat at any one time. Most of the military assigned to Vietnam experienced comfortable living conditions like those at Cam Ranh Bay. Few of them would encounter the experiences of infantry soldiers in combat operations that awaited me.

Oftentimes, family and friends complain that returning Vietnam veterans never talked about their experiences. I happen to believe that sometimes it was because they had nothing to talk about; they never saw action in Vietnam, and wanted to forget or were ashamed to talk about their behavior in a war zone. Prostitutes, booze, and drugs were available on a daily basis to troops in Vietnam.

The liquor and cigarette industries used the war to actively recruit future customers. Cigarettes were provided free of charge to every soldier. They were included in daily rations. A liter of Crown Royal Whisky could be bought on any military base for $1. Many of the young soldiers who served in Vietnam had never smoked, used drugs, drank alcohol or had sex. Many returned to the United States as chain smokers, drug addicts, alcoholics, and with confused thoughts on the meaning of sex.

After a few days at Cam Ranh Bay, I was flown in a C130 cargo plane to Pleiku, Vietnam, in the Central Highlands; headquarters of my assigned artillery unit. At Pleiku, I attended five days of training and was then assigned to lead three-man patrols outside the perimeter of the sprawling base, while waiting for my next assignment. The patrols were dispatched around 3:00 pm and returned the following day around 3:00 pm. On one patrol, we encountered a Vietnamese man pushing a bike loaded with bags. We had been briefed that there should be no Vietnamese in the area we were patrolling and to consider any encounter as hostile. Bicycles were used to transport rice and other supplies to the enemy, so this man was under suspicion of being an enemy combatant.

I ordered him to stop and pointed my .45 caliber pistol at his head from a distance of five feet. The soldiers in my patrol told me to blow his head off. They wanted to see their fearless leader demonstrate a cold ruthless heart. They were disappointed when I allowed him to continue on his way. I had no interest in killing an unarmed man who may have been bringing food to his family. After Vietnam many soldiers suffered severe emotional issues because of guilt about the things they had done in Vietnam.

After a few days at Pleiku, I was taken by helicopter to a small base near the Cambodian border, manned by a company of infantry close to Ban Me Tuyet. I had been assigned to the

4th Battalion, 42nd Field Artillery, 4th Infantry Division. After I reported, I was attached to Company D, 1st Battalion, 22nd Infantry as a replacement for a forward observer whose tour of duty was about to end. One forward observer, normally a lieutenant, is assigned by the Field Artillery to each infantry company.

The responsibility of the artillery forward observer is to call in either artillery or air strikes to support the infantry company during combat. Another responsibility, when on patrol, is to call in artillery just before dark so that the artillery can be adjusted to land close to friendly lines. The men loved to have the artillery called in so that the rounds landed close to their positions. It gave them a sense of security.

Oftentimes, I called the artillery in so close that shrapnel actually penetrated our sandbags. The soldiers enjoyed hearing the shells explode around them. As far as they were concerned, the closer the artillery rounds exploded the better. If the artillery landed close, they knew that the exploding shells would result in lots of dead enemies in the event of an attack, and increase their chances of survival.

I was transported to my new assignment in a helicopter. We left Pleiku for Duc Lap early in the morning. Duc Lap was a Special Forces camp close to the Cambodian border that had been overrun by North Vietnamese soldiers two weeks earlier, resulting in many U.S. casualties. The infantry company I was being attached to had set up a perimeter around the camp, just outside the town of Duc Lap. The perimeter consisted of sandbagged defense positions arranged in a circle. Inside the circle were several open holes for soldiers to use as toilets.

Our helicopter did not land on the small airfield close to the perimeter, which is what I had anticipated. A colonel was on board and was worried about being shot down or worse, getting dirty, so he ordered me to jump out of the helicopter when the helicopter was about 10 feet off the ground. I landed in four feet of mud and had a tough time getting out of the mud hole with my heavy back pack, weapon and combat gear.

I reported to the Company Commander, Captain Allen, who was a 26-year-old, blond, blue-eyed arrogant soldier. After I introduced myself, he pointed to where the lieutenant I was replacing was located and told me to receive my instructions from him. The lieutenant explained that I was to call in and adjust artillery, every night, close to the perimeter, and then informed me he was leaving the next day. Within a few hours of my arrival, Captain Allen barked orders for everyone to follow him and began running across the open field to the wood line. He had received a report that a few hundred yards away an elderly Vietnamese woman had thrown a grenade towards us.

The lieutenant whom I was replacing asked if I was going to go and I replied, "No". I did not believe in following an order that was not based on sound judgment and a plan. The captain had not provided a plan on how to pursue the potential enemy, except to run into the woods and engage the lady with deadly force. He gave the order to charge across an open field and that order was not acceptable to me.

I asked the lieutenant if he was going and he also said "no". This was the first of several times I would ignore the orders of Captain Allen, despite the fact that he was my commander and a senior officer. I attribute surviving my first tour of duty in Vietnam to my refusal to follow orders unless they were based on well-developed plans and sound judgment.

There were many overly aggressive "gung ho" leaders in Vietnam. Some of them were selected by their followers for elimination in a ritual called "fragging". When soldiers felt that a leader was going to get them killed or acted like their lives didn't matter, they would sometimes plan to kill him, by shooting him in battle, or by throwing a grenade at him while he was asleep. These deaths were always classified as "killed in battle", when in fact, they were murders.

One night, while visiting my artillery unit, I was told to stay away from where a certain individual planned to sleep. I concluded that some soldiers must have been planning to execute the battery commander, a captain, while he slept. I reported it to the captain and he took precautions. He was not liked nor respected, and in a combat zone, it's important to your survivability to be liked and respected by your men.

On my second day with the infantry company, we were bombarded with mortar rounds. Like everyone else, I took shelter in a makeshift bunker even though it was not capable of taking a direct hit. Several large mortar rounds exploded close to our bunker, causing it to partially cave in. I adjusted my helmet thinking my experience in a war zone would end that day. I expected the next round to be a direct hit on our bunker that would kill us all.

I had no fear at the time, nor would I ever experience fear during combat operations. I was taught well at Army basic training at Fort Ord and at the Fort Benning Officer Candidate School to resist feelings of fear and demonstrate courage. I met many soldiers who cried and were fearful of being at war. The average age of the military in Vietnam was nineteen. I was almost twenty-four and was more mature and had more military training than most young soldiers. I wanted to be at war, unlike most Americans serving in Vietnam. I had experienced a hostile environment when growing up in poverty and during military training and those experiences had helped prepare me for combat.

When facing possible death in battle, I never gave much thought to the effect my death would have on my wife and one-year old son back home. I don't think soldiers should focus on what would happen in the event of their death. I always focused on the mission, and on making decisions in a way that, hopefully, would minimize casualties and injuries to my fellow soldiers.

My responsibility to the men in my unit was always my first priority. I wanted to survive the war and I took action such as removing rank from my uniform and not following dumb orders. A study of wars clearly illustrates that the enemy targets officers first. Sometimes, I was reprimanded by senior officers for not wearing my rank, helmet or flak vest; but never for being intoxicated, which was deemed acceptable.

My infantry company had the nickname, "Regulars, by God" earned in the Battle of Chippawa, when U.S. Infantry were mistakenly identified as Militia, until they held their lines under British artillery fire. My unit, a reconnaissance unit, had to wear black scarves to differentiate us from other units. Our usual mission was to go out ahead of other units to find the enemy. However, we were given a mission to protect a Special Forces unit at Duc Lap, a recently established base that had been attacked two weeks before I arrived.

The area had received a lot of rain so we slept on rain soaked ground under a relentless monsoon. Our living conditions were very austere. Two guys would pair up and use their ponchos to make a tent that would shelter two soldiers. It often rained in South Vietnam, so we spent a lot of time in our makeshift poncho tents when not out on patrol. It was cold in the evenings in the mountainous region of the Central Highlands. We each carried a light weight blanket and a mosquito net. We always lay down to sleep wearing all our clothes and boots, and holding our rifles on our chests. We lay on air mattresses and covered ourselves with mosquito nets to protect us from the millions of mosquitoes that wanted to feed on us. We had to be ready to defend ourselves at all times and be ready to kill the enemy before they killed us.

My tent mate was Private Barney Reuteman, an 18-year-old soldier from Arizona. His job was to carry a radio for me so that I could call in artillery or air strikes when needed. Barney was one of those guys who had never consumed alcohol, used drugs or had sex before duty in Vietnam but when we parted ways a few months later, he had accumulated all those experiences and more.

All during the night, rats, some over a foot long, would crawl all over our bodies as we tried to sleep, which was not a feeling one desired. Barney had a difficult time dealing with the rats. He would often stay up all night fearful of the rats. One morning, as it was getting light, Barney had finally passed out from exhaustion. Half of his body was outside the tent and half inside the tent. He had no idea that the rats were crawling all over him. He had tried to stay up all night to fight them off, but ran out of energy. I could not help but laugh at Barney that morning.

Our food consisted of C-Rations. There were very few varieties and they tasted terrible unless they were heated. Sometimes we received heating tabs to heat the rations, but most of the time we ate our rations cold. When we went on a patrol we were given a case of C-Rations to pack in our backpack. To reduce the weight in our packs, we would throw away about half of our rations. I threw away things like pound cake, because it was so hard you could play baseball with it, and pork slices that smelled rotten as soon as you opened the can.

We had to pack the canned C-Rations in socks so that their metal cans would not make clinking noises in our packs. Every time we filled our canteens, we had to add disinfectant pills to make the water drinkable. We also had to take malaria pills every day. Many soldiers, including myself, did not always take them because they gave you diarrhea.

We never carried soap or deodorant on patrol because we were trained not to use them unless we wanted the enemy to smell us a mile away. To keep our loads light, we did not carry a change of clothes except for our socks which we had to change every day and we needed for packing C-Rations. Every three weeks, a helicopter would drop off a load of clean fatigues in the jungle for us to exchange. They always seemed to drop too many extra-large sized fatigues and I always ended up with them. At 5'8" and 135 pounds I needed a size small. The problem with the extra-large fatigues was that once they got caked in mud, they became heavy and reduced mobility.

Sometimes, I would send my radio operator, Barney, to the main base in a helicopter to purchase bottles of Crown Royal or Beefeater gin. He would pick up soda for himself and return in a few days on a supply helicopter. While he was gone, I had to carry his radio but it was worth carrying the extra load in exchange for a supply of whisky, gin and toilet articles. There were a few times in Vietnam that other soldiers and I entered combat with the enemy while intoxicated. Fortunately, the Army learned from the Vietnam experience that combat and alcohol do not go together, and it now forbids the consumption of alcohol in combat zones.

When on patrol in the jungles of Vietnam, we were almost always wet from the persistent rain. Our bodies became very dirty and covered with mud. Often we were on patrol for several weeks in the jungle, without a shower, and wearing clothes and boots 24 hours a day. On one occasion we had a chance to use a shower in the village of Ban Me Tuyet. I washed with soap for 30 minutes, but when I stepped outside I noticed I was still dirty. I went into the shower several more times and even after about three hours of showering, I still could not remove the ground-in dirt that had penetrated my skin.

When we went on patrol, our infantry company would often circle a village at daybreak and search for enemy combatants or weapons. Sometimes, the enemy would engage us on patrol, which would result in actual combat. During one such patrol, when Captain Allen, as usual, had not discussed his plans for engaging the enemy, one of the platoon leaders contacted me and requested artillery fire. I began preparing to call in a massive artillery attack on our left flank, a position where the enemy was engaging us with small arms fire.

Seconds before I gave the order to fire, I noticed one of our platoons in that area. If I had given that order, many of our own soldiers would have died. This is an example of how the failure of a leader to plan, and precisely communicate that plan to others, can result in unnecessary casualties. During this contact with the enemy, I observed a soldier who appeared to be aiming his weapon at one of our unpopular platoon leaders from behind. When I confronted the soldier, he denied he was aiming at the lieutenant. I did not believe that I could prove a case of fragging, so I did not pursue the incident, except for informing the lieutenant he may have been a target.

Another mission given to our company was to conduct air assaults on an enemy position. This involved our company of about 150 men, loading up on helicopters, flying to a landing zone (LZ) and fighting our way out of the choppers and into the wood line. Sometimes when we landed, we did not come under enemy fire. When we did come under enemy fire, it was considered a "hot" LZ.

Experienced soldiers, who wanted to survive this type of operation always wanted to sit on the edge of the Huey helicopter, which is designed to carry about twelve soldiers. They knew that the helicopters were the first target of the enemy when landing in a hot LZ so they wanted to be the first out of the helicopter. Oftentimes, the helicopters did not land and the soldiers had to jump a few feet to the ground.

As one of the leaders in the company, I felt it was my duty to be in the front of the attacking force, so I wanted to be on the edge of the helicopter door with my feet hanging out and lead the attack. When I first tried to take that position on the helicopter, the other soldiers would not make room for me despite of my rank. They knew from experience that your chances of survival are better if you're one of the first out of the helicopter. I was determined to place myself in a better position to lead, so when a soldier refused to move, I struck his leg forcefully with the butt of my rifle, forcing him to move and make room for me at the door. I never again had a problem mounting a position at the door on a helicopter to lead an attack. Another lieutenant in the company, Lieutenant Twentymen, used the same technique I had, because he too, felt like he needed to be in the front of the attacking force. On one mission, he was shot in the leg, but the bullet went clean through. He refused to be evacuated because he did not want to leave the combat zone. A medic put some bandages on his wound and he remained with our unit.

After the hot LZ mission, our company was given a mission to fly into Cambodia, which was an illegal operation because it was a sovereign country. Our mission was to locate the headquarters of a North Vietnamese Army unit. The mission was to last for only one day. We landed in an area of Cambodia that turned out to be safe, in that no one fired at us. We patrolled the assigned area and did not encounter the enemy. At the end of the day, Captain Allen called for the helicopters to extract us. Just prior to the helicopters extracting us, the captain was informed that a Sergeant Murray was missing.

The captain decided to stay back, with his radio operator, to look for the missing soldier. He did not order me to stay with him. However, there is a tradition in the Field Artillery that requires that the forward observer always stays with the company commander. When everyone else in the company flew out, I remained with the captain and his radio operator.

The helicopters took the company back into South Vietnam. The captain, his radio operator, and I, began our search for Sergeant Murray.

Captain Allen began yelling out for Sergeant Murray. I pleaded with him to stop shouting and informing the enemy where we were located. Eventually he stopped yelling out for Sergeant Murray. After about two hours, Captain Allen stopped and began taking off his combat gear. I asked him what he was doing. He said we were going to spend the night where we had stopped to rest as it was getting dark. I told him that was not a good plan since according to our briefing; we were surrounded by elements of the North Vietnamese Army. I informed him that I was going to follow a trail for two miles, cross the border, and try to find one of our outposts inside the border. He insisted we follow his plan and I decided to follow my plan. I wished him good luck and started down the trail. His radio operator preferred my idea and followed me. The captain relented and followed meekly behind us.

In the jungle, moving at night time is a challenge because you are moving in total blackout conditions due to the jungle canopy and torrential rain. We had been briefed on the location of the outpost and made contact with them via radio. They were on a hilltop and it would not be easy to find them in the conditions.

The leader of the outpost was familiar with the trail we were on. He agreed to have his men form a human chain by holding hands and reaching out for us on the trail. Luckily, we found them. It was a very emotional moment for me because twenty soldiers on a mountain top, in the pouring rain, in a combat zone, linked their arms together to reach down a trail to help save the lives of their fellow comrades.

The men in the outpost had put up two-man tents by using their ponchos. We did not have our poncho gear with us because we were on a one day mission so they shared their two-man tents with us. The only way three of us could fit was to sleep sideways in a tent barely big enough for two people. I ended up having to sleep on a stump pushing into the side of my body in the middle of the makeshift tent, but at least it was dry and safe. We were three oversized peas in a very narrow pod.

The following day, we thanked the men and left in the helicopter sent for us. I learned a few days later that the outpost was overrun and sadly, everyone was killed.

As for Sergeant Murray, we were informed that he had fallen asleep when we had taken a rest break and had not realized when we departed the area. When he tried to find us, he ran into an ambush. Evidently, we took one fork in the road and the ambush was waiting for us on the other fork, the one that Sergeant Murray had taken.

After being captured by the North Vietnamese Army he was going to be taken to North Vietnam. His shoes were removed so that if he escaped, he would not get far. Sergeant Murray did escape and after ten days of roaming the jungle, he ran into a U.S. Army patrol. It is Army policy to send captured soldiers back to the U.S. because if they were captured again, they would face retaliation. Sergeant Murray returned to the U.S. soon after he linked up with the patrol that found him.

When we returned to our camp, we were sent on another mission to patrol and search a village. Our infantry company surrounded the village before daylight. The villagers began moving around at daylight and noticed our presence in their village. We went into their living areas to search for weapons and found none.

After the search of the village operation, we were given another mission to protect an artillery unit that had been positioned on a mountaintop. We were to build some bunkers with sandbags on the perimeter in order to defend the unit if attacked. The artillery unit was flown in by air. The base was not accessible by land; all supplies had to be flown into the base.

Supplies were normally sent in with a Chinook helicopter which is capable of carrying fifty soldiers, as well as supplies and artillery shells. They were also used to bring in a water tank filled with 5,000 gallons of water. The Chinook has two large propellers that kick up a lot of dirt when landing and taking off and were often called "shithooks". The top of the mountain was often covered with a cloud of dirt, which landed on us and became embedded in our skin and hair.

The priority in resupply was ammunition for the howitzers. We would not be resupplied with food or water very often. There was once an entire week when we did not receive any water for over 250 men on the base.

One day, when we were begging for a resupply of water, a helicopter landed that we hoped carried water. Unfortunately, the helicopter was only carrying the star of a TV series, Tarzan, who wanted to visit the troops. No one on the mountain was interested in meeting him, and in fact, we were angry, because he had not brought any water with him.

Because of the shortage of water, we were not required to shave. However, I shaved every day because it made me feel better. I shaved for two weeks with the same water, kept in my steel helmet, which I used as a shaving bowl.

For Thanksgiving 1968 a helicopter arrived with the traditional food served on Thanksgiving. We were all tired of C-Rations and were looking forward to some real food. Unfortunately, they had forgotten to bring paper plates. Soldiers in Vietnam were not given mess kits like they were in previous wars. C-Rations do not require mess kits and mess kits make lots of clanking noise in your backpack. We were told to bring a container for the Thanksgiving dinner. The only containers we had were our steel helmets and that is what we used to collect our dinner. Fortunately, we had recently received a water supply, so I washed out my helmet for the dinner and, afterwards continued using it for shaving.

During the weeks that we defended this base, there was no direct contact with the enemy. However, we did know that they had soldiers probing our defenses. On a few occasions, we received some incoming mortar rounds. The firebase was out of range for all artillery weapons except for the 175 mm howitzers. These howitzers had the longest range of all artillery weapons in Vietnam but were not accurate. Although I did arrange for them to fire every night, I kept the rounds landing far from our perimeter because they could easily destroy our position because of their inaccuracy.

While on this mission, we had two new replacements: Lieutenant Adams, who became a platoon leader; and a low ranking infantryman, Private Gardner. Lieutenant Adams was a Mormon and always wore his long sleeved underwear despite being in the sun all day in temperatures exceeding 100 °F. Private Gardner was not psychologically prepared for war. He was always scared and his behavior was erratic. At night he would scream out, giving away our position and unsettling his fellow soldiers. Lieutenant Adams, who was his platoon leader, asked me to counsel him. Gardner always looked shell-shocked. I insisted that Captain Allen send him to Division Headquarters (located on a large base close to Pleiku) for a psychological examination. At first Captain Allen resisted, but eventually sent Gardner to be examined. Two days after leaving our firebase, Gardner was declared "fit for duty" and returned to us.

Our next mission involved another patrol. During that patrol, Private Gardner went berserk and starting screaming while manning a position on the perimeter. Lieutenant Adams came running over to me to tell me that Captain Allen was going to kill Private Gardner. I ran with him across an open field and observed the captain running towards Private Gardner and also jamming a round into the chamber of his weapon. I tackled the captain and knocked him to the ground as he yelled that Gardner was going to get us all killed. I asked him to give me five minutes to get him to stop yelling. He was angry but agreed.

When I approached Private Gardner, he was lying down on the perimeter of our small base with one of his arms hidden under a poncho. I quietly began to talk to him about some monkeys that we had seen a day earlier. He looked me in the eye and appeared to be shell-shocked. As I continued my small talk, I noticed his arm coming from under the blanket and reaching out towards me and quickly realized he was about to hack at me with a machete. Fortunately, Lieutenant Adams saw it first and pulled me out of harm's way. The next morning, I again convinced the captain to send Gardner for an examination by a psychiatrist but, two days later he was again returned to us—fit for duty.

My last mission with the infantry company was to secure a very large base in Kon Tum that had previously been occupied by a brigade with over 2,000 soldiers but was no longer in use. It was a massive complex for 150 men to guard. The mission lasted a few weeks. The captain assigned two men to each of the bunkers, which were spread far apart. If an assault had occurred, we would not have been able to organize any coordinated counterattack because of the separation of the bunkers. I spent the day walking the perimeter, and at night, calling in artillery as a defensive measure in the event of an attack.

One evening, just before dark, I observed a soldier in one of the bunkers taking aim at a Vietnamese farmer tending his fields. I believe he had every intention of killing the innocent farmer and I reprimanded him for pointing his weapon in that direction. In Vietnam, the rule was that any man, woman or child killed was definitely Viet Cong or a North Vietnamese soldier.

On another evening, I noticed several soldiers climbing over a barbed wire fence that enclosed the base with a very large box. I decided to secretly follow them to learn what they were doing. The box turned out to be supplementary supplies. The Army provides each unit with one box for every 100 C-Rations issued to a company. The box contains cartons of cigarettes, cigars, pens, writing paper, candy, and other goodies. The soldiers were going into a nearby village and trading the box for prostitutes.

They returned to the base with about six prostitutes and took them to a tent for other soldiers to engage in sex for a price. I also learned that not only were all the officers aware of the situation, but they also allowed it to continue in exchange for free access to the prostitutes. When I went into the tent, I noticed that Lieutenant Twentymen, who had been shot in the leg, was having sex with one of the prostitutes. I heard him announce that he was going to have sex with every prostitute there, as a condition of allowing the situation to continue.

Private Gardner went berserk again. I was called to the bunker where the captain had his headquarters and asked to help with the situation. I decided to try to calm him down by putting on a bit of an act. I slicked down my hair and replaced my shirt with a purple silk robe that I had bought in town that day. I always carried a martini glass, olives, toothpicks, gin and vermouth in my backpack, so I fixed a martini and went over to him. I guessed that by acting relaxed, holding a martini and wearing a purple silk robe I would be able to calm him down. He was so taken aback by my appearance that he stared at me as if I was the crazy one. He did calm down and, again, we sent him to the rear the next day for another psychiatric evaluation.

I asked Captain Allen for permission to accompany Private Gardner to Pleiku so that I could talk to the psychiatrist about his behavior in the field. He gave me permission to be away from the firebase for 24 hours. I met with the psychiatrist and told him that we had sent Private Gardner to be examined on three separate occasions and he was always returned to us fit for duty. I explained that he was a danger to himself and others.

He explained Catch-22 to me, which is that you have to be crazy to fight in a war, so there was no reason for Private Gardner to be removed from the combat zone. I pleaded with the psychiatrist to have him reassigned to the main base but was unsuccessful. After I left Kon Tum, I was informed that the base was attacked by a large force, and that in the end, Private Gardner performed his duty by firing his machine gun at the enemy and was killed defending his fellow soldiers.

A few days after this incident, we had the opportunity to stand down for a few days. We were given permission to leave the combat area and travel to a secure base, take showers, receive clean clothes, eat hot meals, get drunk and or use drugs like marijuana.

One evening, New Year's Eve, 1968, during this stand-down, six of the officers from our company and others were sitting in a circle smoking marijuana after some heavy drinking. When the marijuana joint got to me, I just passed it on because I had never had a desire to smoke pot. I was criticized and told that I could die tomorrow in battle and should smoke pot and relax. I told them if I died the next day, I would die with the satisfaction of knowing that I had never smoked pot.

Captain Allen did not appreciate the way that I would challenge his authority. When he was offered a replacement for me, he gladly accepted. I was promoted to first lieutenant and reassigned to Pleiku as an executive officer with a company that had multiple missions. I was assigned to teach artillery to incoming replacements, supervise a sniper platoon and a special reconnaissance platoon. The special reconnaissance platoon was given special missions by Division G-3, Major Haas.

Major Haas, who was soon to be promoted to lieutenant colonel, believed that our patrols were unsuccessful because we always moved into our night time ambush positions before darkness fell. He believed the enemy was aware of our tactics and he wanted to change them. He ordered our reconnaissance platoon to move into the ambush position after dark and he chose a Lieutenant James to lead the platoon. The lieutenant had received a battlefield commission after receiving a silver star medal for killing numerous enemy soldiers in close combat.

Lieutenant James had what I estimated to be an 8th grade education, and possessed few, if any, leadership qualities. He required repeated instructions as to how his patrol was to conduct an operation. After observing his behavior, I believed he would most likely behave ruthlessly in a battle with no regard for life or property. On his first patrol, he followed the new tactic to move into position after dark. He set up an ambush with Claymore mines with about 30 men.

I was overseeing the operation via radio communication. He informed me that a group of about 40 Vietnamese were approaching his ambush site. I told him to confirm that they were the enemy and not villagers. He failed to follow my directions and executed the ambush with lethal results. Everyone caught in the ambush was killed. According to Lieutenant James, they were unarmed civilians. However, according to policy in Vietnam, they were all Viet Cong, because they were dead.

I immediately informed the Division Deputy G-3 Major Haas that in my opinion a war crime had been committed by Lieutenant James. The next day we went by helicopter to the site of the ambush and found no bodies. Since there was no evidence, there was nothing to report to the commander.

Either we were given the wrong location for the ambush or the bodies had been moved or buried. Lieutenant James suffered no consequences. I never learned what happened to the lieutenant after I left the unit, but judging by his style, I doubt he survived Vietnam.

Major Haas respected my leadership attributes and asked me to join him on several combat missions by helicopter and serve as an air forward observer. On various occasions, I called in artillery strikes from the helicopter for ground units under attack. He was impressed with my ability to deliver artillery on a target while flying in a helicopter that was being fired upon. He started bragging about me and telling everyone I was the best forward observer in Vietnam. He directed me to fly on many more missions where I called in artillery from the air. I went on so many missions that I was awarded several air medals.

On one occasion, he asked me to conduct an investigation of a field infantry unit commander. The Division had received complaints that the commander was forcing his soldiers to march around on a mountain top in 100 °F heat carrying backpacks until they passed out. There were also reports of enemy soldiers being decapitated and their heads mounted on poles outside the commander's bunker. On top of that, it was alleged that he would have his helicopter fly low over Vietnamese civilians so that he could shoot them in the back.

When I arrived at the commander's headquarters, the colonel (sporting a haircut as though he was trying to look like a Mohawk Indian) immediately ordered me to stand at attention. He reprimanded me for carrying a Thompson submachine gun ("Tommy Gun") and wearing a jungle hat instead of a steel helmet. He was angry that a lieutenant was sent to investigate him and told me he was going to have me court-martialed for being out of uniform and carrying an unauthorized weapon. After he calmed down, I began my investigation by interviewing the troops under his command.

The colonel acknowledged that he did have them march all day on the mountain top in the heat. One young soldier cried the entire time I interviewed him. I had previously met him at Pleiku when he went through training. I knew he was scared to be in Vietnam. Only one soldier confirmed that there had been (at one time) some decapitated heads in front of the commander's bunker, but they had been removed. Some soldiers also admitted that they had observed the commander shooting from the helicopter but said that he was shooting at the enemy.

When I returned from the investigation, I provided a written report. Since I had experience being in combat and on many patrols, I understood the need for the commander to keep the soldiers in shape. Sergeant Murray, who was captured on one of my patrols, was not in great shape, which is why he was so tired and fell asleep. As far as the other concerns, I just reported on what I had learned from my interviews.

After giving my report, I went over to see the psychiatrist and asked him to intervene on behalf of the struggling young soldier I had interviewed. I reminded the psychiatrist about Private Gardner, who I had referred to him many times earlier and who was killed in action. He did send for the soldier and after his examination, assigned him to a job on the base that was less stressful and more secure.

Pleiku, headquarters of the 4th Infantry Division, was located in the Central Highlands of Vietnam. The Army base included an airfield, barracks, Base Exchange (which is a retail store) as well as cafeterias, chapels, hospitals and other facilities normally found on a military base in the United States. The area is also the home of the Monte nards, a tribal group that was discriminated against by the Vietnamese.

They were uneducated and not allowed to attend schools. Their average life expectancy was only 40 years. Many of them had lost their teeth by the age of 30 due to chewing betelnut opium. They lived in thatched, one-room huts built on poles. They subsisted on rice and, sometimes, fish. The females in the tribe did not wear clothes above the waist when it was warm.

I wanted to learn more about these tribal people, so I began walking alone off the base into their village. Sometimes, I did not take a weapon. Verbal communication was impossible, as they did not speak English and I did not speak their language. So I began to communicate with them nonverbally and established a relationship with some of them. Sometimes, I squatted down with them just to observe other villagers, smiling with them when they smiled and acting surprised when they did. Eventually, they allowed me to take pictures, which was a rare privilege. They did not allow others to take pictures of them because they believed pictures captured their souls. They were a gentle people who smiled often and appeared to be at peace with their lives.

Major Haas heard of my contact with the Monte nards and asked me to try to purchase six of their houses. He wanted to set up a Monte nard village on the base in order to train new replacements. The Monte nards always burned a house after a death because they felt the house held their spirits and the spirits would hurt the village if the house was not burned. Because they trusted me, they sold us five houses over a period of several months, for $400 each.

One day while on base and driving in a jeep to visit the Base Exchange, I observed a soldier lying on the ground bleeding profusely. There were other soldiers standing around him. The injured soldier had accidently discharged his large caliber rifle (M14) and the bullet had torn his leg open. The surrounding soldiers acted like they wanted to watch him bleed to death.

I immediately removed the injured soldier's belt and used it as a tourniquet to stop the bleeding. My jeep driver and I placed him in the jeep and rushed him to the base hospital, where he was treated and later medically evacuated to the United States. Oftentimes, the Army goes overboard with awarding medals. Although I did not feel deserving, I was awarded an Army Commendation medal for my actions in saving his life.

At that time, soldiers were allowed to have one week of rest and recuperation (R&R) after serving six months in a combat zone. Married soldiers were allowed to travel to Hawaii to meet their families. Vyone met me in Hawaii for my R&R. Our son remained in California with his grandparents. We had a great vacation together on the beaches of Hawaii. We had both lost a lot of weight in the six months we had been separated by war. Vyone did not ask questions about Vietnam. We had been exchanging letters several times a week so she was aware of what was going on with me in Vietnam and me with what was going on with her and Jim. We still have those letters we sent to each other. I returned to Vietnam refreshed and ready for another six months of duty.

A few months later, I was given the opportunity to take another week of R&R. I was given the choice of going to Thailand, Taiwan, or Australia. I selected Taiwan as I had always had an interest in Chinese history. Soldiers who went to the R&R locations often went for a week of sex with prostitutes and binge drinking. I had no interest in either of those activities. On arriving in Taiwan, I was surrounded by prostitutes who wanted to be my partner for the week. However, what I wanted was a native islander who could show me the island and explain its history.

Out of frustration, I asked a young English-speaking native Taiwanese female, who was around 20 years old, and worked in a bookstore, to be my guide for a few days. Initially, she resisted because she believed that everyone would think she was a prostitute when they saw her with an American soldier. She eventually accepted my proposal and turned out to be a great tour guide. We took the bus to many scenic and historical areas in Taiwan before I returned to Vietnam.

Most single and married soldiers had engaged in sex on these R&R trips or with Vietnamese prostitutes in Vietnam. Many of them contracted sexually transmitted diseases (STDs). One of our outstanding sergeants, Sergeant First Class Rodriquez, was one of those soldiers. One day Sergeant Rodriquez received a letter from his wife and went berserk. After reading the letter, he grabbed his rifle and began firing indiscriminately in the barracks at Pleiku.

After taking his weapon away, we learned that his wife had contracted an STD from him while they were in Hawaii on an R&R trip. To her, the STD was proof of her husband's infidelity. She had filed for divorce, which caused the Sergeant to go berserk.

During this tour of duty, I was called on to serve on a jury that court-martialed soldiers who committed crimes or violated Army regulations in Vietnam. One court martial involved a black soldier who had refused to obey an order from a white officer and had gently pushed him. Apart from me, the court martial board consisted solely of white senior officers (majors, lieutenant colonels and a colonel). I was the only junior officer (a first lieutenant) on the board. After hearing the case and finding him guilty we deliberated on the sentence. The chairperson, a colonel, of the court martial board insisted on sentencing him to twenty years in prison and a dishonorable discharge. Others present suggested sentences from five to twenty years. I recommended six months in jail with no dishonorable discharge. The chairman immediately berated my recommendation as being far too lenient and stated it would never be approved by the board.

We each took a turn to justify our recommendation. My justification was that the soldier was provoked by the officer into reacting in the manner that he did. We began to take votes on each sentence that was recommended. Surprisingly, we reached a majority vote on my recommendation. The chairman immediately announced that it was not a valid vote and that we had to vote again.

I challenged his decision and stated that the vote was valid and that he did not have the right to call for another vote. I demanded he call in the judge for instructions. The judge stated that if everyone agreed to vote again, we could vote again. I refused to vote to take another vote. My punishment recommendation was the sentence approved for the young soldier.

Near the end of my tour of duty, my youngest brother Larry asked for my assistance in obtaining a transfer to Vietnam from Korea. Larry, who was twenty, informed me that he was serving with the Army in Korea and was in trouble and needed to get out of the country immediately. I went to the personnel office on the base and asked for them to help him obtain an assignment to the 4th Infantry Division with me. They arranged his transfer and he arrived at Pleiku. His duty was to drive a diesel truck and resupply units on the base with fuel. Drivers were only armed with rifles. I felt he needed a pistol so I gave him a .45 caliber pistol that belonged to our unit.

Our schedules and locations kept us from seeing each other more than three times. On his second visit, he attended an awards ceremony, at which I was awarded several medals including the Bronze Star, several Air Medals and an Army Commendation medal. When my brother returned home after his tour of duty, he would tell family members that he was supposed to have received the medals but I used my rank to take them away from him. When Larry told these stories about Vietnam, he was an alcoholic and it is important to understand that he created these falsehoods as an alcoholic. He eventually stopped drinking and recognized that he did not mean to say these things.

There were many politicians and celebrities who visited Vietnam to help lift the morale of soldiers by demonstrating that they cared about us. One of the celebrities I met and took a picture with was Martha Raye. She was an actress but was more successful as a comedian. She had spent more time in Vietnam with the troops in the field than any other celebrity or politician. I met her again later in Austin, Texas, where she was performing in a dinner theater. I sent the picture of us taken in Vietnam backstage and she invited Vyone and me to go backstage and meet her. We hugged and talked about Vietnam and how life in general was going for all of us.

Major Haas had been promoted to lieutenant colonel (LTC). As the end of my tour of duty was approaching, he asked me to become his artillery liaison officer (ALO). He was scheduled to take over an infantry battalion and was authorized to have an ALO, who is normally a captain. I respected LTC Haas and agreed to extend my tour of duty by six months, but only for that position. The division artillery commander called me into his office and said he would not approve my transfer because the job called for a captain and I was just a lieutenant. I decided not to extend my tour of duty since I did not know what I would be doing for the next six months and because I would not be able to work with LTC Haas.

A few days before my tour of duty was over, I had to send out a routine patrol from the reconnaissance platoon in our company. One of the sergeants begged me not to send him out on the patrol because he only had a week left on his tour of duty and was afraid he would be killed. Soldiers close to their rotation date are very superstitious about doing anything dangerous. Sergeant Smith had tears in his eyes as he pleaded with me.

However, it was his turn to go and I had to order him to go on the patrol. I wanted him to feel safe so I decided to go on the patrol with him, even though I had only a few days left myself. He stopped tearing up and we had a successful patrol.

I returned to the United States a few days later and reflected on my experiences in Vietnam. I accepted the fact that my actions as a forward observer, ordering tens of thousands of highly explosive artillery shells to explode, most likely resulted in the death of the enemy as well as innocent civilians. I often reflect on my role in the war and my actions which resulted in the death of fellow human beings. I also remind myself that the death of innocent civilians happens in every war.

After returning from Vietnam in September 1969, I was promoted to captain and was given the command of an artillery battery at Fort Carson, Colorado Battery B, lst Battalion 19th Field Artillery. I was very proud of the promotion when it was announced in September. I was 24 years old and felt I had come a long way from being a high school dropout. I received the orders with an effective date of promotion in early December.

On the day I should have been promoted, the battalion commander had not scheduled a Promotion Ceremony. I was too excited to wait and decided to wear the double silver bars, sometimes referred to as railroad tracks, signifying the rank of captain. The commander was not happy when he found out and told me to take off the captain bars until he decided to have the ceremony.

Military duty in a peaceful environment was not as rewarding as duty in a combat zone. As a commander, I felt a great responsibility to treat the young soldiers with respect and fairness as we trained for war. Up to this time in my military career, I had not learned to have a lot of respect for the noncommissioned officers (NCOs) in the Army. NCOs are the sergeants who actively supervise low ranking enlisted men. They often demanded that I punish soldiers under their supervision for minor infractions. As a battery commander, I had authority to determine the guilt and inflict punishment on soldiers under my command.

Sergeants would often demand that I reduce in rank, administer a fine, give restrictions, or assign two weeks of extra duties or all of those punishments to those who were subject to their orders. I felt that sergeants were abusing their authority and were using me to punish soldiers for personal reasons. Sergeants would demand the maximum punishment for soldiers who would tell a sergeant, "Fuck you". It seemed to me there were too many young soldiers saying such things to the sergeants and perhaps some sergeants were not being truthful about these confrontations with their men. Commanders are often pressured to support the recommendations of their NCOs. If they are not supported, then they blame all discipline problems on the commander for failing to support them.

I decided to call a meeting of all the sergeants in my unit and discuss this issue. First, I told them if a lower ranking soldier said "fuck you" to a sergeant there had to be a respect problem. I believed that sergeants should accept some responsibility for a soldier using profanity towards them because it was evidence that they had no respect for the sergeant. I explained that respect was a two way street and had to be earned and not demanded. I notified them that in the future they were to counsel any soldier who used profanity towards them and determine what they could do to earn that soldier's respect. The NCOs, all of whom were older than me, became angry when I informed them I would no longer punish a soldier for using profanity towards a sergeant. I told them I would meet with any sergeant and offending soldier to help them determine how they could work together more effectively.

They all decided to protest against my decision to the battalion commander, a lieutenant colonel. They complained to the colonel that I was refusing to back them up, and without my support they could not lead their men. They demanded that I be replaced and if I was not replaced they would all volunteer for Vietnam duty. I did not back down from my decision.

The sergeants stopped bringing the lower ranking soldiers to me for punishment and morale increased significantly in my unit. The colonel only mentioned the complaint to me when visiting our unit but did not indicate any concern over my policy. After all, we needed volunteers for Vietnam.

Fort Carson, along with other Army bases, continued to experience racial problems. There were several race riots on the base. Whenever there was an uprising, unit commanders would call in the military police and there would be violent confrontations between black and white soldiers. On one occasion, an Army sedan carrying a white colonel was stoned as it entered the area where the uprising was occurring. The Post Commander and Commanding General, Major General Bernard W. Rogers, was becoming frustrated at how his leaders were dealing with the race problem on the base.

General Rogers ordered all his commanders not to call the military police when there was an uprising. Instead, he directed the leaders to manage the uprisings and use their command authority to quell any disturbance. He also ordered that officers on duty who performed checks on the barracks at night stop carrying side arms and CS grenades.

CS grenades are used to dispense tear gas to break up riots. These were decisions made by an outstanding leader who would later end the dreaded KP duty for soldiers by hiring civilians to perform those duties. He also ended the routine of 6.00 am formations for the entire Army when he became Chief of Staff of the Army. Later in his career, he was selected to serve as the Supreme Allied Commander, North Atlantic Treaty Organization (NATO).

Soon after the general's decision, I happened to be the officer on duty and had to check the barracks after a major fight occurred between blacks and whites. I entered the barracks alone wearing civilian clothes and without a weapon or CS grenades. The glass in the entrance of the barracks was shattered. White soldiers were running out of the building with bloody faces saying they had been attacked by blacks. As I walked the halls of the barracks, I observed black soldiers playing cards and acting as if nothing was happening. The black soldiers treated me with respect and answered my questions. I did not call for the military police, but did give a report to my unit commander.

During my tour at Fort Carson, there were demonstrations all over the country against the Vietnam War. On one occasion, a large group of demonstrators arrived at the gated entrance to Fort Carson. One of the leaders of the group was Jane Fonda. General Rogers picked her up at the gate, gave her a tour of the base and then returned her to the entrance to the post where she was later arrested. At social functions attended by senior officers, including generals, there was much discussion as to who in the military was supporting the movement to end the war. Some were concerned about expressing their true feelings because they believed that they would be considered disloyal and have their careers ended prematurely.

Nine months after returning from Vietnam, I again volunteered for duty in Vietnam and was given a reporting date of September 1970. Later, my wife would tell me that she could understand why I volunteered the first time for Vietnam. She felt that I had to get it out of my system. However, she never understood nor accepted my volunteering and placing myself in harm's way a second time for duty in Vietnam. I was initially assigned to the 4th Infantry Division. However, the division was returning to the United States because the war was winding down.

By 1970, our government had decided it was time to begin a gradual withdrawal from Vietnam and was returning military units to the U.S. a few at a time. Consequently, there was very little activity in our division. We had five captains assigned to one position. Some of them were seeking an early return to the U.S., whereas I was seeking another assignment that would keep me in Vietnam. After about a month, I was reassigned to the 5th Battalion, 4th Artillery, in support of a separate infantry brigade of the 5th Infantry Division on the border of North Vietnam.

My duty was to serve as the battalion fire direction officer for the brigade. The responsibilities of this office were to verify the computation of data from the artillery batteries assigned to support our brigade, and most importantly, to approve the command to fire on targets.

Another major duty was to determine which targets to fire on, based on the guidance of the commanding general, who at the time was Brigadier General Hill. There were two fire direction officers so that there could be one on duty at all times. We each had a 12-hour shift, seven days a week, in the control center of the Battalion Fire Direction Center. The battalion and brigade were located in Quang Tri province, very close to the border of North Vietnam. The brigade was in a relatively quiet area which resulted in very few engagements with the enemy for the first five months of my assignment. Quang Tri was like Pleiku, providing most of the comforts of a large military base in the U.S.

After about five months of duty in Vietnam, I was given a week for R&R in Hawaii to relax with my wife and son. The vacation was very enjoyable, especially with my son Jim being able to join us this time. He was almost three years old and very mobile. He was so mobile that he managed to fall off a small bridge into a man-made creek near a shopping mall. I immediately jumped in after him, only to find that the water was only two feet deep. We both ended up quite wet but shared a special moment that day in Hawaii. I returned to Vietnam believing that I would have another seven months of duty before returning to the U.S. However, upcoming events would prevent me from completing my full tour of duty in Vietnam.

Daily life in Quang Tri was so boring that a young sergeant who had the duties of a forward observer started discussing with me how we should end the war early. He frequently went out in a helicopter to monitor activity on the border. Sergeant Hudson told me he wanted to call me when he was in the air and direct us to engage targets in North Vietnam. He had this totally unauthorized plan to start a battle with North Vietnam on their soil so we could end the war.

At the time, the policy in Vietnam was that we were not allowed to fire into North Vietnam unless fired upon. He informed me that he was going to stray across the border, cause the North Vietnamese to fire on his helicopter, and then request us to respond with artillery fire.

The field artillery battalion commander happened to walk into the control center and wanted to know what was going on. When I explained that a forward observer was requesting fire support in North Vietnam he directed me to refuse the request. Soon after this failed effort to get the war moving, the brigade was given an order to leave Quang Tri for Khe Sanh and support a major operation involving 100,000 South Vietnamese troops. The highly secretive operation was called Lam Son 719. It would be the last major combat operation involving American soldiers in Vietnam.

Operation Lam Son 719 was a joint operations plan that required the South Vietnamese Army to go into Laos and destroy elements of the North Vietnamese Army, which had occupied an area in Laos near the border of South and North Vietnam. Our forces were not allowed to cross the border but they would support the South Vietnamese Army with artillery and air power. Several other American units, including elements of the 101st Airborne Division, moved into the area to provide security for the roads and additional artillery weapons to support the operation.

Several years prior to our arrival, Khe Sanh had been the site of a military defeat for the Marines. The Marines had been sent to Khe Sanh to secure a large airfield. In a major confrontation, they were surrounded by North Vietnamese soldiers and eventually forced to retreat from Khe Sanh. When we arrived, the base had been deserted for a long time. The brigade set up its headquarters close to an airstrip. A massive bunker complex was built to house the brigade headquarters. Our vehicle had a tent extension and was set up close by to control the artillery in the area. All artillery units in the area had to obtain clearance from us to fire on any targets.

Again, my military experience and survival instincts came into play. Most of the soldiers slept in the open and when we received incoming mortar or artillery shells, which occurred frequently throughout every day, they would run to a reinforced bunker. There were not enough bunkers for everyone to take cover. I did not like the idea of working a 12-hour shift and then having to get up frequently to run and look for a bunker so I decided to build my own shelter.

I dug a hole six feet deep, three feet wide and six feet long to be my place of rest when not on duty. On top of this hole, I placed scrap iron and four rows of sandbags. I figured I could survive any artillery or mortar attack except for a direct hit on my personal bunker and sleeping quarters. Fortunately, because of the season we did not receive too much rain so my hole did not have a problem with water seepage. I located a cot and placed it in the hole so that I would not be sleeping on the ground. I often woke up to find scorpions all around me, but they never bothered me and I never bothered them.

When I had free time, I would listen to a tape cassette sent to me by Vyone. In spite of my request to send more tapes, all I received was a tape of Burt Bacharach. I listened to that tape so much that I learned the words to all the music, but more importantly found the music a quiet distraction from the war around me.

The other battalion fire direction officer assigned to the unit liked to be called "The Greek" because his family was from Greece. Captain Marek rotated 12-hour shifts with me. He chose to sleep in the open but always complained he never could sleep when he was off duty. We were supposed to be supervised by Major Gurr, the Battalion S-3, who was a West Point graduate. However, we rarely saw him in the control center. Major Gurr was another officer with few leadership qualities. On one of the rare occasions when he was in our control center, we were under an artillery attack. Major Gurr ordered us to get under the tables in the tent extension. We all ignored him and crowded into the light armored vehicle. During the operation, he was relieved of his duties because the Battalion Commander, LTC Ridgeway, was not satisfied with his performance of duty.

The brigade set up a mess hall to serve hot food. Except for the constant bombardment and extreme heat, living conditions at Khe Sanh were not too bad. During the day, we would observe helicopters heading to Laos to support the battle plan. Hundreds of them were shot down and air-lifted from Laos to a base in South Vietnam. Almost every night the commanding general would come into our control center and point out targets that he wanted us to attack with thousands of rounds of artillery. It was my duty and the duty of the other battalion fire direction officer to coordinate the engagement of all of those targets by the artillery in the area and give the approval to fire. Sometimes, targets of opportunity would occur and we would engage actual enemy forces.

On one occasion, we received a call for fire support from a forward observer in a helicopter. He stated that the target was over one hundred vehicles that included howitzers, personnel carriers and trucks. We were ecstatic and prepared to attack the long convoy of vehicles. We soon learned that these were actually vehicles the U.S. government had provided to the South Vietnamese Army. The South Vietnamese Army had abandoned them. We had no choice but to destroy millions of dollars' worth of U.S. Army vehicles.

On another occasion, we were given a report that a helicopter had been shot down on the border and that several bodies lay close to the downed helicopter. The commanding general decided not to attempt recovery of the bodies for several days because he had received orders that no U.S. soldiers were to enter Laos except by air. Most of us were angry that there would be no attempt to immediately recover the decaying bodies and we felt that the general was being ruthless and did not care about the dead soldiers.

A few years later, I had the opportunity to interview that general, now Major General Hill, when he was assigned as the Deputy Commanding General of Fort Hood. Prior to my interview, a news article appeared concerning General Hill's efforts to work with boy scouts and other community organizations. In the article he was portrayed to be a very caring person. I asked him how he could ignore the retrieval of the rotting bodies of American soldiers at Khe Sanh and yet be so caring and helpful to others. He had no good explanation except to say it was war time and things are different in war.

Operation Lam Son 719 was the largest military operation ever conducted by the South Vietnamese Army in the history of the war. It was their opportunity to demonstrate what the U.S. President was saying, which was that South Vietnam was capable of continuing the war without the help of the U.S. government. The secret operation was a total failure and proved that the South Vietnamese army was not ready to assume control of the country. In April 1971, the operation came to an end and the brigade was ordered back to Quang Tri.

I volunteered to have our operations center be the last vehicle to leave Khe Sanh so that we could control the artillery and air support necessary to cover the exodus of 5,000 plus American troops. Our operations center was down to one armored personnel carrier (APC) and four men including me. When we left Khe Sanh, we were a lone vehicle loaded with four soldiers. We had no security assigned to protect our withdrawal.

Our route took us along a dirt trail for about ten miles, with high ground on both sides, before arriving at a hard top road that would lead to our destination. The vehicle's intercom was not working and the driver did not know the route to Quang Tri. I positioned myself on top of the APC so I could tap the driver on the head to direct him on which way to turn. The driver was in a protected driver's compartment just below where I was sitting. Two other men were inside the vehicle in the passenger area.

As we neared the hard top road, we observed a narrow river. I decided to stop our vehicle so we could all bathe, because none of us had taken showers in months. While two of us bathed, the other two provided security. When we finished, we provided security while the others bathed. After our break, we climbed back in (and on) our vehicle and departed. We arrived at the hard top road about thirty minutes after our break. The hard top road was on fairly level ground that went through an open area. Our fears of being attacked eased since there was no longer high ground on both sides of the road. The driver, who had been traveling at about fifteen miles an hour on the dirt trail, began to accelerate the APC. We were all anxious to get back to the base and happy to be on a hard top road, even in the open which seemed safer than the dirt trail.

After about fifteen minutes, the driver began to shout but I could not hear him at first because of the engine noise. I yelled down and asked what the problem was. I finally heard him yell that the steering on the vehicle was not working and I quickly noticed our vehicle was starting to leave the road and go over an embankment. I immediately envisioned myself being thrown from the vehicle, run over and killed by the tracks on the twelve-ton vehicle. Unlike those inside, I had no protection from being thrown from the vehicle.

The vehicle was moving at about twenty-five miles an hour, which is fast for an armored track vehicle. I was about twelve feet from the ground when I decided to jump. I landed feet first on the hard top road. In an instant, I had made the decision to jump, rather than be thrown and possibly crushed by the tracks on the vehicle. Fortunately I was wearing my helmet which stayed on until the last roll. I also was fortunate that my side arm, a .45 caliber pistol which had a round in the chamber did not go off and put a hole in my leg.

When my body finally stopped rolling, I was conscious and was not in any serious pain. I felt paralyzed from the waist down and had some bruising on my head and arms. Within about 30 minutes, a helicopter carrying LTC Ridgeway landed and evacuated me and the others to the hospital and Quang Tri. As a result of losing steering, the APC had veered off the road and over an embankment. The vehicle came to an abrupt stop, which caused two soldiers inside the vehicle to be injured. The driver sustained no injuries. The two soldiers inside the vehicle had one open fracture each.

LTC Ridgeway visited me in the hospital and I told him I would be back to work in a week and wanted to be selected to command a battery in the battalion. He told me that he had planned to assign me to command a battery but it would depend on my medical situation. At the hospital, the doctors said they had completed x-rays of my body and could find nothing wrong. I was not able to stand on my feet or walk.

The Doctors told me there was no reason why I should not be able to walk. Hospital staff made several attempts to have me walk, but to no avail. Finally, they decided to x-ray my ankles, which they had overlooked. They found that I had fractured both of my ankles. The decision was made to medically evacuate me to Japan for surgery. Two months after the accident, my battalion was ordered to return to the United States as part of the plan to withdraw from Vietnam.

I was transferred to Japan on a stretcher in a plane designed to transport wounded soldiers. In Japan, I received an operation on my left fractured ankle. A screw was placed in my left ankle to repair the fracture. The right ankle fracture, which was not as serious, would be operated on at a later date. While at the hospital, I witnessed many wounded soldiers with much more serious injuries than mine. Some were burned beyond recognition; others had been shot in the stomach and would be severely disabled for life. Several celebrities visited the hospital. One was the cartoonist for the television program, Casper the Friendly Ghost. He drew a caricature of me while visiting with me.

When soldiers are sent to Vietnam, they complete forms as to who they want to be contacted in the event of death or injury. In the case of an injury, soldiers have the option to elect not to have anyone informed, which is what I had selected. As a result, my family was not aware of my injury until I called them from Japan. I called my wife and told her I was in Japan. She thought I was there on R&R. When I told her I had been hurt and was in the hospital, she immediately began to cry and passed the phone to her father. I explained that my injuries were not serious and that I would have an operation the next morning on my fractured ankle. Vyone had recently learned that her former fiancée of three years had been killed by an enemy mine. She was concerned that my injury was more serious than I was telling her. Her father, a World War II veteran, consoled her and explained to her that I would be sent home after the operation.

When I arrived in Monterey, California in April 1971 from Vietnam, I had to be transported in a wheelchair. The Army gave me a 45-day convalescent leave of absence. Vyone, Jim and I spent the leave in a small studio apartment very close to the beach in Carmel, California. Vyone would often take my wheelchair out of the trunk of the car for my use when we went to the nearby beach. After the leave, I was able to use crutches and was no longer dependent on a wheelchair. At the end of the leave, I received orders to report to Fort Sill, Oklahoma, for a nine-month Field Artillery Officer Advanced Course designed for captains.

My second tour of duty in Vietnam provided me with very different experiences than my first. On one hand, it was not as dangerous as the first tour. I did not have to go on patrol and engage in close combat with the enemy. The experience of being involved in the largest joint operation in the history of the Vietnam War was exciting and rewarding.

On the other hand, I also had the experience, not desired by anyone, to be medically evacuated from a war zone. This experience allowed me to witness the emotional and physical damage inflicted on those severely wounded or injured in a combat zone. On my first tour, I returned with many emotional experiences that result from being in close combat. At the end of my second tour I had to face a lifetime of living with a disability that would restrict my mobility.

Lexington, VA, 1968. Four generations of the Author's relatives: (clockwise from left) Son (James), Author, Aunt (Martha), Mother (Nancy), Aunt (Tina), Aunt (Mary), and Grandfather (John Harvey Smith).

South Vietnam, 1968. Author's "poncho tent".

Duc Lap, South Vietnam, September 1968. 2nd Lieutenant Kimball and Private First Class Barney Reuteman, returning from a reconnaissance mission.

Kon Tum, Vietnam, 1969. Author with Monte nards in their village.

Fort Carson, CO, December 1969. Captain Kimball (24), Commander, Battery B, 1st Battalion, 19th Field Artillery, 4th Infantry Division.

CHAPTER FOUR

Race Riots and Corruption in the Army
(1971-1978)

Fort Sill, Oklahoma is the Army's center for training soldiers in Field Artillery. In 1967 I had been assigned to Fort Sill to attend the Field Artillery Officer Basic Course, which is designed for new lieutenants. In 1971, I was enrolled in the Field Artillery Officer Advanced Course, which is designed to train Army captains for high level staff duties. When I began the course in June, I was on crutches and in a foot cast, however, I had it removed after the first month of classes. Vyone and I rented a three-bedroom, two-bathroom house in Lawton, Oklahoma.

In those days the city of Lawton had a bad reputation because of the many prostitutes in the city that arrived on payday weekends to service the soldiers on the base. Downtown Lawton was not a place to visit with the family in the early 1970's. However, we had many family outings to a nearby wildlife refuge and to a park on Mount Scott. Over time the city leaders managed to clean up the city, and today it is a great place to serve in the military with a family.

Prior to my arrival at Fort Sill, the Army had begun to downsize, as the war in Vietnam was coming to an end. For officers, the reduction in force targeted Army captains, some of whom did not want to be released from the Army. Of course, most of the draftees were looking forward to receiving their discharges. The end of the Vietnam War required the Army to remove over 5,000 captains from their ranks. I recall many friends receiving unsolicited orders notifying them that their service in the military had ended. Captains who held the status of regular army officers were not subject to the reduction in force. Officers who had graduated from the military academies were given that status. Officers who had graduated from a University's Army Reserve Officers' Training Corps (ROTC) program and were in the top 10 percent of their class were also given that status. During the Vietnam War, approximately 90 percent of the captains in the Army did not have the status of regular army and were classified as reserve officers, like me. We had entered service from the National Guard, Army reserve, or officer candidate schools, and were the officers subject to the reduction in force. Many of us considered this to be unfair.

Prior to my arrival at Fort Sill, the Army had released several lists of names, captains who were being discharged as part of the reduction in force. I wanted to make the Army a career and did not want a "pink slip" (a notification that my services were no longer needed in the Army). When we began the nine-month course, we were all told we would not be subject to the reduction. However, after the course was in session for one month, another list was published and many of my fellow students were on it. Luckily I survived the downsizing and was never given a pink slip. I attributed my retention in the Army to a combination of my college education, combat experience and command experience. Many of the captains who were forced to resign had neither college degrees, nor command experience.

Our training was primarily scheduled to take place during the day time, which gave us time in the evenings and weekends to spend with our families. I enjoyed the training but wanted to return to studies at a university. Fortunately, the training schedule allowed me enough time to do both. I enrolled in a program leading to a Master of Arts degree from The University of Oklahoma.

The university had an extension program that held classes at Fort Sill. I also completed some of the courses on the university's campus in Norman. Other courses were offered in other cities, where you could earn three credits by attending a class that met for eight hours a day, six days a week.

The Master's Degree Program was designed for students to major in "Human Relations". The department chair was Dr. George Henderson, who would have a profound influence on my future. He was an African American, slight of build, who taught from his heart. He taught me how to become an effective change agent and to seek self-renewal often. I later achieved success in bringing about change as a community activist because of what Dr. Henderson had taught me.

His class presentations often required students to consider the question of whether or not we are our brothers' keepers. We participated in role playing exercises to explore the true meaning of empathy. Dr. Henderson always made it clear in his classes that it was each individual's decision as to whether or not you are your brother's keeper and that he would not influence that decision for any of us.

The program helped reinforce my belief that I am my brother's keeper. I decided to further dedicate myself and the skills I had learned, to helping others. The program emphasized how education leads to knowledge and the acquisition of skills. One day, Dr. Henderson told us that some professors wanted to place restrictions on who was admitted into the program. They were concerned about students with unethical agendas acquiring the knowledge and skills to become change agents. They believed that receiving a higher education and developing such skills results in great power, which could be abused.

We studied the histories of most ethnic and cultural groups in great detail. I quickly became aware of the historic struggle and oftentimes, hopelessness of many minority groups in our country. One of the books we read was, "Educating the Powerless" by Stanley Charnofsky. This memoir, Guns, Books and Lawsuits summarizes the lifelong commitment I made at that time: to dedicate my future to helping the powerless acquire knowledge through education and other learning experiences.

I think the professors who wanted to place restrictions on who should be allowed to enroll in the program were partly correct. Education and learning human relations skills does lead one to understand power. However, understanding power alone is not sufficient. An effective change agent requires courage and needs to take responsibility for helping others bring about change in their community.

The Master's program and the Army's training provided many opportunities for self-analysis of my strengths and weaknesses. Although I had spoken to small groups when I was 19, I had never felt comfortable speaking in front of large groups, so I decided that acting in a community theater might help me build up confidence.

The Lawton Community Theater was a theater-in-the-round, where seats encircled the stage. When I auditioned for the comedy, "A Thousand Clowns" I never expected to be selected for a part because I had no acting experience. However, the director selected me to play the brother of the main character. During the first performance, in a scene where I spoke to someone on the phone, I forgot my lines, and very loudly said "shit", which was obviously not in the script. The audience roared with laughter, which helped me to relax and remember my lines. My experiences in Community Theater would help me become more confident, persuasive and credible in communicating and bringing about change in my future endeavors.

The Master's program, the Army's training course, and Community Theater involvement occupied much of my time, leaving less time for my family. However, we did take time to go to parks on weekends, and entertain other officers and my brother who visited from New Hampshire. My brother Danny was struggling with chronic alcoholism. He was not able to find work, nor keep his family together.

I arranged for his travel to Fort Sill, hoping I could help him. However, soon after he arrived, he became demanding, belligerent and negative. For instance, he demanded a case of beer every day and at one time had 10 cases stockpiled in the garage just for his consumption. On one occasion, I had a cast party for those in a theater production. Some of the cast members were children so I asked my brother to drink outside because he was being disruptive at the party.

I later learned that Danny told other family members that I had thrown him out of the house and made him sleep in the backyard with the locusts that plague the area in the summers. It was not unusual for such stories to be made up and passed around my family to discredit me. Despite this, I returned to New Hampshire nearly every year, for many years, to try to help my brothers and sisters. The only way I felt I could really bring about significant change for them was to move back to New Hampshire and give up my Army career. Instead, I chose to do the best I could from afar.

In the fall of 1971, the State of Oklahoma held a lottery for hunting elk on a wildlife refuge near Lawton. The refuge had to cull the herd because of excessive numbers. At the time, I enjoyed hunting and fishing so I decided to put my name in. I won one of the three hundred licenses to kill an elk. During the hunt, I saw a running elk, over 500 yards away. I tried to shoot it, but not being a good marksman, I did not expect to hit it. The elk darted into the woods and I assumed I had missed.

Fortunately, a park ranger heard the shot and made me search where the elk went into the woods, and we found the animal. She had been pregnant, and was dead, along with her calf. We transported the elk to a butcher shop and our family ate venison for six months. That experience led to a decision: I never wanted to hunt or kill an animal again. I sold all my hunting weapons and never killed another animal.

During my training at Fort Sill, I had a desire to write and attempt to publish an article. I wrote an article for the Field Artillery Journal, and to my surprise and great joy, it was published. The article considered the idea that if we use artillery fire to create unsafe air corridors for enemy aircraft, the aircraft's ability to inflict damage would be reduced. Having an article published for the first time was very exciting and motivated me to attempt to publish further articles in the future.

Around this time, Vyone and I began discussing having another child. In May 1972, we learned that she was pregnant and we would have another child in December. Unfortunately, we did not know what we now know about the dangers of drinking alcohol and smoking cigarettes when pregnant. Vyone continued to smoke and drink, socially. Fortunately, our daughter did not have any health issues when she was born.

A month before completing the Field Artillery Officer Advanced Course in April, I learned that the Army was assigning me to Fort Hood, Texas. I was not pleased with the assignment because I felt there would be no action. I attempted to get out of the assignment but to no avail. However, the assignment turned out to be very fortunate for us. We learned to appreciate the great state of Texas and would eventually make it our home.

Before heading to Fort Hood, we took a 45-day vacation and visited New Hampshire. We rented a three-bedroom cottage on Squam Lake for thirty days. The cottage was right on the lake, very quiet, and had few distractions. It did not have a television or telephone. While on vacation, I continued research for my Master's thesis on the family known as "the buggies", the very large family that used to be our neighbors when I was a child. They were still being harshly treated by the community in Nashua. The Mayor told me that my thesis helped him gain funds and assistance for the family. Completing my thesis was the final requirement for my Master of Arts degree in 1972.

In June that year, we drove to Texas and arrived at Fort Hood and began looking for a house. We wanted to buy a house, rather than rent one. We also did not want our children growing up in Killeen, the city just outside of the sprawling base, because of a soaring crime rate. We decided to buy a house in the quiet town of Belton, which was twenty miles from Fort Hood. We found a house that needed a lot of work, but we were prepared to do it. It was a one-story house, probably built in 1910. The house had not been painted in at least thirty years. Paint was peeling inside and outside of the three-bedroom, one-bathroom house.

The house was on a corner lot on Penelope Street in Belton. We painted the outside of the house bright yellow, with a black trim around the doors and windows. Today, in 2011, it still has the same color scheme. We also painted every room inside the house, unknowingly exposing Vyone to dangerous chemicals during the sixth month of her pregnancy. Our daughter, Kathryn

Penelope Kimball, was born on my birthday in December 1972. Her middle name was taken from the name of the street where we bought our first house in Belton.

A few months before she was born, my mother came out to visit us for six months. She was single and actually went on a few dates with a neighborhood gentleman. She enjoyed taking our son for walks in the small town and caring for the new baby. Our Christmas was special that year because of our daughter's birth and my mother sharing our home in Belton.

After we completed some renovations on the house and enrolled our son in a pre-kindergarten class, I reported to Fort Hood and received an assignment as one of several G-3 division operations officers, with the 2nd Armored Division (known as "Hell on wheels"). In January 1973, former President Lyndon B. Johnson passed away after a heart attack. Our division had plans in our files for his funeral. We had been provided the plans because some of our units would be used to provide security. Few of the details in the plan were actually implemented, because the grieving family changed many of the arrangements.

Our family drove from Fort Hood to Austin to participate in the funeral on January 25, 1973. At the time, our daughter was only a month old but we decided to take both children with us. Our family waited in line in the bitter cold for over two hours to view the former President lying in his casket and to pay our respects.

My duties as one of the division operations officers consisted of developing plans for maneuvers and updating top secret contingency plans for the division. Whenever the division (consisting of about 15, 000 men and women) moved to the field for a major exercise, I would plan how and when each unit would move and return to the base. A division usually has three brigades as well as division artillery. The Field Artillery Commander, Colonel Akers, expected me to give his units special treatment because I was an artillery officer and should be looking out for them.

He figured that after my one year of duty as an operations officer I would be looking for a job that would advance my career, and therefore I should please him. When I did not show favoritism, he was not happy. When I inspected one of his units and reported to the commanding general that they were poorly trained, Colonel Akers was determined to end my career.

The colonel made it clear that I would never be given command or any worthwhile assignment when I was assigned to his unit. Fort Hood had two divisions on the base. I quickly obtained a guarantee that I would be given a command in the other division, the First Calvary Division.

Despite this, Colonel Akers was able to exercise his authority and have me transferred to his unit. He assigned me as an assistant operations officer with one of his battalions. He directed my soon-to-be supervisor, Major Marc Cisneros, to run me out of the Army by any means. Fortunately, Major Cisneros (who would later become Lieutenant General Cisneros) took a liking to me. He often told me that at that time I was the only officer who worked for him who he felt was totally honest and had a sense of integrity. Major Cisneros would eventually be influential in my career: firstly, in my selection as a battery commander (over the objections of Colonel Akers); and again later, in my selection as a battalion commander.

The injuries to my ankles in Vietnam prevented me from running long distances. I knew that to be competitive in the combat arms (Infantry, Armor, and Artillery), I had to be able to run long distances and keep up with soldiers during our daily physical fitness exercises. I sought elective surgery to correct a problem in my right ankle that caused pain when I ran. After the surgery at the Fort Hood hospital, I was able to run long distances again, which I believe, saved my career in the combat arms. The surgery would also allow me to participate in a sport that I would enjoy immensely: downhill skiing.

In the fall of 1974, as part of a community fundraiser held on a local television station, we placed the highest bid in an auction for a week in a condominium in Vail, Colorado. We drove there with our two children and took ski lessons for the first time. My son and I did well with our lessons and after a few days were able to go to the top of the mountain and ski all the way down. We both fell in love with skiing and would continue to refine our skills in Europe and other U.S. ski resorts. When I assumed command of a field artillery battery, I had to live in a house on the base due to Army policy. We had to sell our house in Belton, but were fortunate to sell it for twice what we paid for it. The house on the base was newer, but much smaller. Unit commanders work long hours, but by living on the base and avoiding a 35-minute daily commute each way, I was still able to spend time with my family.

Throughout the 1970s, the Army continued its struggle with race relations. The Army had officially begun integration in 1948, when President Harry S. Truman signed in a law that ended segregation in the military. However, the last unit was not integrated until 1954. In the early 1970s, black soldiers were still not treated fairly in the Army. They were given punishment more often than white soldiers. While the Army had policies that prohibited discrimination, they only influenced a soldier's behavior and not his attitude. There is a major difference between behavior and attitude. While behavior can be monitored by policies and laws, attitudes cannot. The majority of white soldiers had deeply-held racial prejudices. These prejudices were predetermined attitudes toward blacks that were not based on facts.

There were very few black noncommissioned or commissioned officers in the Army. They were spoken to in ways that made them feel inferior. The Army felt it was necessary for every unit to appoint a "Race Relations Officer" to mediate in any race problems in the unit. Army units would typically assign the duty to a new lieutenant, fresh out of college, who had no real authority or credibility. The Army also set up Race Relations Courses (also called Sensitivity Training) to help soldiers understand how to work with minorities and treat them fairly.

While serving as a battery commander, I was asked by black soldiers to be the battalion's race relations officer. They knew I was in a command position and would have access to the unit's leadership and could voice their concerns. I accepted the position and wore a name tag above the "U.S. Army" label on my shirt that read "Race Relations Officer". The executive officer of our battalion, Major Merchant, was a southerner and did not support my decision to take on the assignment.

One complaint that I took to Major Merchant was that the soldiers did not have a working water fountain in their barracks. He quickly responded that the water fountains were on order and that was all he could do. I told him that there was a working cold-water fountain outside his office that was only serving a handful of office staff. I told him that if he did not have it moved to the barracks by the next day, there would be another riot. He looked at me as if he wanted to exterminate me on the spot. I felt like I was back at Fort Benning in the 1960's where whites killed other whites for being so called "nigger-lovers".

Major Merchant was furious that I would threaten him with a race riot if he failed to act on my request. Commanders who failed to control race riots or had too many discipline-related incidents were subject to removal, along with some of their staff. The next day, three cold-water fountains were installed in the barracks and his fountain remained outside his office. He would later include a few negative comments in my performance report.

Our unit had a lieutenant who was extremely prejudiced against blacks. The black soldiers had no respect for Lieutenant Erwin and planned to assault him. One night he was the duty officer; and as he was going down a staircase, he was struck in the head with a brick and knocked unconscious. The next day, I advised Colonel Lydall (the battalion commander) that if he did not enroll the officer in a Race Relations Course, he would have a riot on his hands. The black soldiers were demanding he be sent as a condition not to riot.

The lieutenant was defiant, and begged the colonel not to be sent to the course. The colonel took my advice and sent him along anyway. If the colonel had any more riots in his barracks, he would most likely have been relieved of his command. Major Cisneros, the Battalion S-3 at the time, would tell me later that my actions regarding race relations may have saved Colonel Lydall from losing his command.

In the 1970's, the Army determined that it had not recruited enough soldiers to serve in the combat arms. The Army changed the career field of many soldiers from non-combat arms to Infantry, Armor or Artillery. This policy required intense training for these new recruits, who had already received training in other fields. My unit was selected to train the soldiers in the field artillery, at a small compound on the northern most edge of the sprawling base. The training went very well, and within a few weeks, the new recruits were performing all the duties of field artillerymen. Some of the howitzer crews were totally manned by the new recruits.

On one occasion, Battalion Commander, LTC Lydall went out to the field to check on my unit and the training. When he arrived, he found all six self-propelled howitzers and vehicles practically abandoned. I had left only a few guards, and had taken the other 130 soldiers to go swimming. I had promised my men that if they did well, we would all go swimming at a nearby lake resort.

I always believed that if you take care of your men, they will take care of you. The temperature was over 100 °F and the men deserved the outing because of their outstanding performance of duty. When the battalion commander arrived at the lake, he was quite surprised by what he found, given that we were supposed to be training. However, he was the type of leader who gave his total support to his commanders and backed their decisions.

Our battalion had five units called batteries. Each battery consisted of about 150 men and was led by a captain who was the battery commander. During the summer of 1974, the officers of our battalion were selected to help train the National Guard at a camp in Mississippi. Several states had sent soldiers to train at the camp, including Kentucky. At the end of the training assignment, we were each given a certificate stating we were officially a "Kentucky Colonel" (an honorary title given in recognition of public service for the State of Kentucky).

During the training, we had a lot of free time on the weekends. One weekend, the five commanders (including myself) were all playing cards. Soon the discussion turned to racial jokes and slurs. I quit the game protesting that they were prejudiced. I admonished them for being in a command position where they had the power to punish soldiers. I argued that if they felt that way about blacks then they should not be in command.

The four other officers tried to make light of their jokes and racist slurs, but I would not accept that. Unfortunately, in the early 1970's, this kind of behavior was typical of most white officers. I once had a conversation with a Korean War veteran who told me that if a black soldier left a foxhole or attempted to run from a battle situation, he had standing orders to shoot to kill and blame the enemy,. Although the Army ended segregation in 1948, it had not achieved equality in its ranks by the 1970's.

The commander of our division, 2nd Armored Division, was a Major General Robert Fair. He was very ambitious and made every effort to gain attention so that he would be promoted. Race relations was not one of his priorities. He was only interested in gaining an outstanding reputation in the Army. His changes to division policies were like a return to the days of General Patton's command at the beginning of World War II.

He ordered parades be held every Friday with a lot of pomp and ceremony. General Fair had a siren placed on his jeep, just like General Patton, who wanted his troops to know when he was in the area. Like General Patton, he carried the insignia of rank for enlisted men and would promote a soldier on the spur of the moment to prove how powerful he was.

General Fair was determined that our division would have the best record in the Army. To achieve this, he decided our division would have the lowest number of soldiers who were absent without leave (AWOL—a serious problem in the Army at the time). He directed his brigade and battalion commanders to stop reporting soldiers as AWOL, because, he argued, they would all eventually return to duty. Our division soon had the lowest number of AWOLs in the Army. The policy was totally illegal, because as soon as soldiers cannot be accounted for, they are required to be reported AWOL immediately.

One of the brigade commanders, whose father had been a famous general, who was also expecting to be promoted to general, almost lost his military career because of this non-reporting policy. The brigade commander, did not report soldiers AWOL (as directed by General Fair) and unfortunately, three weeks after one of his soldiers could not be accounted for, he was found dead in a ditch. There was a major investigation by the Army and the policy was changed at Fort Hood.

In spite of his lack of integrity, Major General Fair was promoted to lieutenant general and assigned command of V Corps in Germany, which consisted of about 70,000 soldiers. A few months after he took command, a brigadier general reported Lieutenant General Fair to the Army for making illegal and inappropriate changes to policies. After an investigation by the Army, after only five months General Fair was relieved of his command and became the first commanding general officer to be relieved of his command in Europe since World War II. General Fair retired, moved to San Francisco, California, and died less than a year later.

In 1974, the news of the Watergate scandal and impending impeachment of President Richard M. Nixon dominated conversation among my fellow soldiers. We often discussed the news articles and rumors that the President might try a military takeover of the government, suspend the Constitution and end the powers of the U.S. Congress. Just prior to the announcement of his resignation, our division was on a very large field military exercise at Fort Hood, Texas. We were ordered to stop all military maneuvers and return to base. As we rode back to base, I thought about what I would do if the rumors were true and the President did attempt a military takeover. I recall making a decision, without any hesitation. Although we take an oath to obey the orders of the President of the United States, I decided I would desert the Army and join any resistance movement to oppose a military takeover.

When joining the military, every soldier is required to take an oath to obey the orders of the President and the Constitution of the United States. I had no doubt that defending the Constitution took priority over anything else. If President Nixon attempted a military takeover, I had every intention to immediately send my family to Canada and remain behind to fight with the resistance. Fortunately, because of his resignation I was never required to act on my commitment to our Constitution.

Army promotions had slowed down in peace time. During the Vietnam War, an officer was promoted to captain with less than three years of service, which is one of the reasons why the Army had too many captains after the war. I had been promoted to captain in December 1969, but had to wait nine years to be considered for another promotion.

In 1975, after completing my second command I was given orders to report to Houston, Texas. I had been assigned to Reserve Officers' Training Corps (ROTC) duty at the University of Houston. The ROTC assignment required officers to serve as instructors and mentors to students enrolled in the program. Colleges and universities had to agree to appoint an ROTC instructor as an Assistant Professor of Military Science. The universities required that the officer have a Master's degree.

We decided to purchase a house in the Houston area since the assignment was for a minimum of three years. All the real estate agents we met would ask if we would mind looking at houses in a "salt and pepper" area. They asked that question because they did not want to show houses to white clients who were opposed to living near blacks. We had no objection and decided on a house that was in a predominantly black neighborhood. The house was located in Missouri City, about 20 miles from the University of Houston. The house had five bedrooms and two bathrooms but was less than 1,800 square feet.

We enrolled our son in an elementary school that was predominantly black, without any review of the quality of local schools. We were not aware that his school had a poor record of academic achievement. Today, fortunately, most parents do review the reputation and quality of schools their children attend, which is an absolute necessity. Our son, along with every other child at the school, was not provided an adequate education for the three years he attended that elementary school and had to struggle through high school and college. Failure to review the school's record prior to enrolling him was one of our greatest mistakes as parents.

I taught leadership and tactics to the students at the University of Houston. We also took the students on field trips, where they would sleep overnight in tents. Many of the students were from low income families and were in desperate need of mentors, if they were ever going to graduate. Some of them would sign up for just twelve credit hours and then drop three credits. At that rate, it would take seven years to graduate with a bachelor's degree.

In addition to teaching, we were responsible for helping students succeed in college. On several occasions, I admonished students for their lack of progress. If students had not responded to the counseling and admonishment, they probably would not have graduated.

While assigned to the university ROTC program, I decided to pursue a doctorate in educational leadership. Admission to the doctoral program involved an interview by a committee of professors. I appeared at the interview in uniform and after the interview learned that I was not accepted into the program. Dr. Anderson, a member of the committee, informed me that I was not accepted because committee members believed I would have "tunnel vision" because I was in the military. She protested and advocated for me to have a second interview, after which I was accepted into the program.

I found the course work easy. The military paid for the tuition because I now qualified for the GI Bill as a Vietnam veteran. After one year of study in the program, I requested a two-year leave of absence from the Army so that I could complete my doctorate, before being reassigned to another location. Unfortunately my request was denied, due to my lack of political connections.

On September 19, 1977, Vyone's mother passed away in Seaside, California at the age of 64. She was found lying on the bed in her bedroom with a suitcase half-packed. She had decided to join her husband, who had left months earlier to stay with family in North Dakota. Hannah hated to leave the house she had learned to love and where she felt safe. Sadly, when she finally made the decision to leave, she had a heart attack and died. Vyone decided that the children (who were in school) and I did not need to attend the funeral, so she and her brother Larry traveled to California, to attend the funeral.

In 1975 I became a big brother with the Big Brothers Big Sisters of America organization. Another volunteer and I were assigned two brothers, aged thirteen and fourteen. The children's divorced mother was an alcoholic, without any steady income. They lived in one of the poorest apartments in Houston. Sometimes, the other volunteer and I would take the boys out together to a movie or a camping trip. Other times, we just took the boys out for one-on-one mentoring. The boy I was assigned, Bennie, had a school record that revealed low levels of achievement. I met with his teachers, but they had no advice on how to improve his academic performance.

Bennie had a heart of gold, was carefree, laughed a lot and spent many weekends with our family. He became a big brother to my three-year-old daughter Kathryn and my eight-year-old son Jim. Bennie was always laughing and full of joy in spite of his poor environment. Sometimes, he would spend weeks with us during the summer months. When my assignment ended in Houston in 1978, he insisted we take him with us when we moved away. His mother was opposed to him leaving Houston. Bennie asked us to request a judge appoint us as his guardians so that he could go with us. We never expected the judge to rule against Bennie's mother, but he did and Bennie became a member of our family.

The ROTC program at the University of Houston consisted of a lieutenant colonel, two majors, two captains, two noncommissioned officers and a secretary. Lieutenant Colonel Alvarez was given the title of Professor of Military Science by the university. The colonel was obese, which was permitted at that time. He also lacked integrity and committed fraud during his tenure. He did not appreciate the way that I questioned his decisions and pointed out inconsistencies in his practices and policies.

Colonel Alvarez was from McAllen, Texas, which is on the Mexican border. He frequently traveled to McAllen "to recruit", and always requested travel reimbursement from the Army. However, he never recruited one student and the trips were actually vacations, paid for by the Army. All the staff members would discuss how the colonel was misusing funds but would not take any action. He also used one of the staff members to drive him around on personal shopping trips in a vehicle provided by the Army. Colonel Alvarez had a son in the ROTC program and approved a local ROTC scholarship for him. His son received failing grades in some of his courses. For the ROTC class, which he rarely attended, he received an "A". Hoping that he could keep the others quiet about this practice, the colonel awarded a scholarship to the son of the major who supervised the scholarship program.

I decided to report the colonel to his superior officer, Colonel Alvey, who was based at Fort Riley, Kansas. When Colonel Alvey visited our campus, I told him about the inappropriate actions of Lieutenant Colonel Alvarez in relation to his son, staff, misuse of funds and enrolling students who were not eligible to be enrolled. Colonel Alvey told me in a very stern voice, "You're a captain, he is a lieutenant colonel. Just do what he tells you, he is your commander!"

When I studied the principles of leadership, I learned that a dozen character traits contribute to developing an effective leader. I had always believed that the most important character trait of an effective leader was integrity. Maya Angelou, the novelist, disagreed with me, in that she felt the most important character trait was courage. Eventually, I came to agree with her, because without the courage to expose any lack of integrity shown by leaders, possessing the leadership trait of integrity becomes meaningless.

I decided to prepare a detailed report on the wrongdoings of Lieutenant Colonel Alvarez and other staff members. My plan was to deliver it to the Inspector General of the Army at the Pentagon in Washington D.C. in person. I explained to Vyone that once I turned in the report, I would never be promoted again and would probably be forced out of the Army. The Army had a policy whereby if officers were not promoted in the normal length of time it takes for promotion, they would be discharged. It was called an "up or out" policy. My doctorate studies became even more important, because I had every expectation I would be looking for another job soon.

My three-year tour was due to end in July 1978, and I had not received a follow-on assignment. That summer I was due to be considered for promotion to the rank of major, but was not hopeful of being selected. In June, we left Houston for a thirty-day vacation and visited New Hampshire, as had been our custom between assignments. We rented a cottage on Squam Lake for three weeks and enjoyed spending time together as a family. On the road from New Hampshire to Houston, after our vacation, I explained to Vyone that we were coming to a fork in the road.

One road led to a detour via the Pentagon and one directly to Houston. I told her that I was torn as to which road to take because if I submitted the report it could end my Army career. In the end, I decided to go to the Pentagon and turn in my report. The officer who took my complaint thought I was a disgruntled employee who had received a poor performance report from the colonel. I showed him a copy of my performance report, which reflected a 100 percent score and had all the right boxes checked. Later, Colonel Alvarez would tell students that he thought his outstanding report of my duty performance would keep me silent.

The Army sent a team of senior officers to investigate my complaints. Nine months after I filed my complaint, the Army's Inspector General sent me a report that validated most of my allegations. As a result, the Army took punitive action on some of the staff. They arranged for Lieutenant Colonel Alvarez to retire; they forced one major to resign from the Army prior to his eligibility for retirement; and they allowed the other major to retire as a major. The other captain on the staff was not selected for promotion to major and resigned.

When I returned to Houston, I received military orders that would assign me to a field artillery battalion in Germany. In addition, I learned that I was on the promotion list for major, and would be promoted in December 1978. A few weeks after returning from our vacation, we departed for another vacation and then traveled to Germany to report for our next assignment.

ROTC, University of Houston, TX, 1978. Captain and Mrs. Kimball.

CHAPTER FIVE

NATO and the Warsaw Pact
(1978-1982)

The United States maintained over 100,000 servicemen and women in Europe in the 1970's. The Army had several divisions deployed in Germany, which was part of the North Atlantic Treaty Organization (NATO). NATO was a military and political alliance of nations that was organized to deter the Soviet Union from attacking our allies in Europe. To deter NATO from attacking, the Soviet Union had established its own military alliance, the Warsaw Treaty Organization of Friendship, Cooperation and Mutual Assistance (known as the Warsaw Pact). Member states included Poland, Hungary, East Germany, Czechoslovakia, Hungary, Romania, Bulgaria and Albania. I was assigned to the 2nd Battalion, 377th Field Artillery. The battalion was armed with mobile missiles capable of delivering nuclear warheads on the Warsaw Pact forces, if they decided to attack NATO or any of its allies.

The U.S. military forces in Europe were all volunteers. In 1972, the U.S. Congress passed a law to end the practice of drafting men into the military and began the transition into an all-volunteer military, which took many years to achieve. Salaries of those serving in the military were doubled and many benefits were increased, such as financial support for college education after military service. Standards for entrance into the military were raised. Draftees only had to have a very basic education, whereas volunteers now had to possess a high school diploma. Army leaders serving with troops were directed to change their leadership style so that they would not discourage soldiers from remaining in the Army after their terms of service ended. Unfortunately, many of them did not change their behavior, and continued to treat soldiers as if they had no choice about being in the Army. I wrote about this morale issue and had an article published anonymously in a major military journal in 1980.

The assignment to Germany was the first opportunity for my family to live in a foreign country. My family did amazingly well adjusting to life at a small Army base in a foreign country. Herzo Base was positioned on a small hill just outside the city limits of Herzogenaurach. Nuremberg, a major city in Germany, was only seven miles away. The base had two field artillery battalions and one brigade headquarters. The battalion commander had planned to assign me to command of a battery, but he had to change his plans. The rank required of a battery commander was captain. I was a captain at the time, but was scheduled to be promoted to major in a few months, so would not have been able to complete the normal two year tour of a battery commander.

We were assigned an apartment in a row house on the base. The apartment was old but livable. It was only a four-minute walk from what would become my office in the battalion headquarters. After reporting to the, 2-377th Field Artillery Battalion I learned that another captain had arrived, who was also soon to be promoted to major. The battalion commander, whose wife suggested he was an alcoholic, informed us that he would assign one of us to the S-3, operations position, and the other to the more senior position of executive officer; after he had a chance to observe us. He had more of an opportunity to learn about the other captain because every day at 5:00 pm they went across the street to the officers club and drank to the point of intoxication.

I always went straight home after work because every day we ate dinner together as a family. The battalion commander selected his drinking buddy to be the executive officer, and officially, my immediate supervisor. We did not work well together and I would be reassigned within a year.

My assignment as the battalion operations officer, S-3, would later help my career because I eventually did become a battalion executive officer and would have experience at both levels. As the operations officer, it was my responsibility to plan and supervise all the operations of the battalion. Approximately 600 men were assigned to the battalion. There were five separate units, each commanded by a captain and with about 120 men. Three of the five units had two Mobile Missile Launchers each as well as other support vehicles. The other two units were support units.

We frequently went on field maneuvers in the surrounding area to practice our mission with dummy missiles. Once a year, we went to the island of Crete, part of Greece, to actually fire a missile with a dummy warhead. We were evaluated by a multinational NATO team. If any of the results were less than satisfactory the senior officers in the unit would generally get fired, so there was a lot of pressure to do well. Each of the units with launchers was required to fire one missile each. The firing units rotated to Crete on a weekly basis for three weeks during the summer. I was required to be present for the entire three weeks. The soldiers and I had a lot of free time to enjoy the beaches and the island. These summer visits to the island of Crete were enjoyable and rewarding.

In November of 1978, I was promoted to major at a small ceremony on the base. As a family, we went on many tours of Italy, Great Britain, and other countries. We took ski trips in Austria and within Germany itself. My salary was increased and we had more disposable income, which we invested. The economy in the U.S. was struggling with hyperinflation. American Express owned the banks that serviced the U.S. Military in Germany and they were providing certificates of Deposit that paid 15% interest. We invested approximately one third of our income.

In 1979, on returning from a ski trip, I found a note on the door of our apartment. It stated that I had been reassigned and was to report for duty at the brigade headquarters, as the brigade logistics officer, or S-4. This was not the normal procedure when reassigning officers. I felt it was probably a result of the commander and executive officer making decisions while intoxicated. I learned to go with the flow and settled into my new job.

On July 3, 1979, Vyone's father Alvin passed away at the age of 62, from health issues related to his heavy smoking and drinking. Again, Vyone thought it best that the children and I remain in Germany while she and her brother flew to Seaside, California for the funeral.

That summer, I was scheduled to attend a two-week training session about ten miles from Munich. I took our son with me on the trip and showed him how to ride the train into Munich and how to tour the city on foot. He took the train and spent time in the city by himself on several occasions. He was only twelve years old but quickly learned to do things like this on his own.

The 210th Brigade had four battalions assigned to it with about 2,500 soldiers. I was logistically responsible for supporting the entire brigade. The four battalion commanders were pleased with my duty performance and shared their appreciation with the brigade commander. Unknown to me, one of the battalion commanders at Herzo Base had been asking the brigade commander to reassign me to his command as his executive officer. As a result, in 1980 I reported for duty as the executive officer of the 3rd Battalion, 37th Field Artillery.

Eighteen 155 mm self-propelled howitzers (mobile artillery) and about 700 men were assigned to this field artillery battalion. The Battalion Commander, Colonel Bacheldor, was very aggressive, charismatic, and was considered to be an officer who would be promoted to general someday. He had total confidence in me and we worked particularly well together. The soldiers in the battalion respected his leadership style. When two soldiers were found naked in bed, he had them transferred to units located on separate bases, whereas most commanders would have had them discharged for behaving as if they were gay.

We did have some differences of opinion on how to handle a few situations. For example, when two soldiers got into a fight in the barracks, he would have the two of them forced into a makeshift ring and have them fight each other in front of the other soldiers. All the soldiers in the unit were required to watch the fight. This was not Army policy and I was surprised he got away with it. The policy worked as far as reducing the number of fights. Soldiers did not want to be on public display fighting each other, so conflicts were quickly resolved with words and not fists. However, I felt it was dehumanizing to force one soldier to fight another, in front of men who were sworn to protect each other in combat.

Two or three times a year, our battalion relocated to Grafenwoehr, a large sprawling Army base in Germany, to conduct field maneuvers and practice firing our howitzers for 30 days at a time. We lived in tents, showered in the field under a five gallon can, ate field rations, and spent up to 36 hours awake. They were demanding times, which provided excellent training and prepared everyone for battlefield situations. Most of the 30-day exercises were conducted in inclement weather, often snow or heavy rainfall.

As the executive officer, I had my own vehicle with an assigned driver. On an almost daily basis, I went to a phone booth on the base and called my family to let them know how things were going with me and to check on them. Vyone shared some of these calls with the battalion commander's wife, whose husband only called home once a week. She became upset with him because he was not calling more frequently. When away from home, I always made every effort to frequently call my family to check on them and make sure all was well. It is a practice that I have followed all my life.

In 1980 my 20-year-old niece Valerie, daughter of my brother Fred, contacted me and wanted to visit us in Germany. Her intention was to visit for only a week, but she ended up staying with us for six months. We traveled together to Great Britain, Italy and Austria on self-guided tours. After she left us, she visited a friend in Germany and eventually married him.

In 1982 my mother flew to Germany and stayed with us for six months. We took her to a few interesting places in Germany but she was not up to travel in other countries. I often took her shopping in Nuremberg and Herzogenaurach. I explained to her how and where to buy coffee. One day, I told her I was going to drop her off and let her spend a few hours in town on her own.

She was very fearful of being left alone since she could not read or write English, much less German. When I picked her up from her first solo visit, she was so pleased that she had been able to buy coffee, shop and relax by herself in a foreign city that she went on several more trips like that by herself.

Our tour of duty in Germany had originally been scheduled for three years, but the Army allowed extensions on request. I loved my job, my family loved Germany, and together we decided to add one year to our tour of duty in Germany. The American schools in Germany did not have a good reputation. Our only concern was the fact that our children would have to go to school in Germany for another year.

The Army had some serious issues with families breaking up because of its three-year rotation policy. They decided to make every effort to rotate soldiers between two or three bases to try and keep families together. As a result of that policy, the Army assigned us back to Fort Hood, when my tour of duty in Germany was completed. We were all excited by that new assignment because it meant returning to Belton, the small town in Texas that we loved.

Prior to leaving Germany we contacted a realtor in Belton and explained that we wanted to purchase a large historic house. She provided a list of several and we selected one, sight unseen, and made an offer. The owner did not accept our offer prior to our departure, so at that point we had nowhere to live when we arrived.

On the day we left Germany, we all boarded a bus in Nuremberg for Frankfurt to catch a plane to the U.S. Bennie was the first to start crying. When our son Jim and daughter Kathryn saw him crying, they all began to cry. They were sad to leave Germany, their schools and friends but we all knew it was time to go back home. As was our usual practice between assignments, we took a vacation, this time for 45 days. We drove to New Hampshire and again rented the cabin on Squam Lake for three weeks. The cabin still had no TV, radio, computer or phone. We had opportunities to do things together as a family including hiking, swimming, boating, fishing and visiting our family in New Hampshire.

CHAPTER SIX

Fort Hood and Airborne
Operations in Honduras
(1982-1986)

After our vacation at Squam Lake, we drove to Fort Hood and finally negotiated to buy the historic 1892 Victorian Home on Main Street in Belton. The house had over 4,000 square feet and had a very interesting history. We researched the previous owners and were able to obtain pictures of them, which we displayed in the entrance hallway. We began to attend auctions to purchase antiques to furnish the house.

The house was impossible to keep warm in the winters. Until we added heat sources and took steps to increase the energy efficiency of the house, we often had to wear our jackets and gloves in the house.

Just prior to leaving Germany, I had ordered a new Mercedes D300 from the factory in Germany. It was delivered soon after our arrival in Belton. My family fell in love with the large historic house and the new Mercedes. The children quickly adjusted to their schools and life in Belton. My first assignment at Fort Hood was to the III Corps Operations Center, a crisis center that is manned 24 hours a day, seven days a week and was just down the hall from the office of the III Corps Commander, who commanded over 100,000 soldiers.

I wanted to be assigned to troop duty and was not happy with this high-level staff assignment. This job required me to inspect other Army bases for their compliance with nuclear weapons procedures. The job mostly involved waiting around for a crisis and maintaining a record of significant events. While in this position, I was selected for promotion to lieutenant colonel. After you are selected, you must wait for promotion based on the promotion number assigned. In my case, there would be about an 18-month waiting period.

While serving in this position, I volunteered to be a facilitator at Sensitivity Training. The Army had a long history of using sensitivity sessions to help soldiers adjust to changes in military policies. I had attended them as an enlisted man in the early 1960's. We were shown films of black families living their normal lives in their homes. The purpose of these films was to help whites overcome their prejudices. In 2011, Sensitivity Training has been ordered for soldiers to help them overcome their prejudices against gays in the military.

In 1983, when I assisted with facilitating the sessions, there was no specific purpose, except to keep the doors open between the command and young soldiers. The idea was to bring soldiers together to discuss their problems and issues, and give them an opportunity to raise them with an officer outside of their command structure. I was asked several times by soldiers if they could smoke marijuana in these sessions on an experimental basis. The soldiers wanted to test the command's commitment. I had always been opposed to the use of marijuana and enforced the laws accordingly. However, I wanted the soldiers to know I was open to any requests. I decided to agree to test the attitude of the base leaders.

I prepared a letter to the III Corps Commander requesting his approval to allow the soldiers to experiment with marijuana in the sessions. It was an unlawful request, and as a senior Army officer, I felt I would end up getting reprimanded for making it. However, there were no consequences after all, and of course, the request was denied.

Meanwhile, my son had joined his high school football team. When I learned that he was being harassed at school by the coaches, I decided to confront the school board. The coaches had a policy to paddle students who received grades less than a "B", which was against district policy. The policy clearly stated that corporal punishment could not be given for academic reasons. It also stated that another staff member had to be a witness, and that the punishment must be documented.

None of these policies were being followed when Jim received corporal punishment. I gave a presentation to the school board on the incident and requested that Belton High School follow district policy. It became clear that I was being misunderstood by some present, who acted as though I was opposed to corporal punishment and proceeded to quote related bible scriptures. My son faced even more harassment at school after I raised the issue with the board. However, after my presentation, the district policies on corporal punishment were enforced.

I took another action, this time against the city council, which resulted in my children being further harassed at school. There were rumors around town that Main Street (the street in front of our house), would be widened, and many of us would lose our front yards. I wrote several letters to the local paper, the Belton Journal, about the issue. Based on news reports, it appeared that the city council was in secret discussions to widen Main Street.

The Belton Mayor called and invited me to his house to discuss my allegations. We had a nice chat about the issue, but I was still convinced that actions were in motion to widen the streets. I attended and presented at several city council meetings. The council members and the Mayor appeared to ignore all of my concerns.

I decided to host meetings of others who were concerned over the issue. There were several historical houses on the street, including ours, that would be impacted by widening the street. I convinced those present at the meetings that we should begin a petition to recall all members of the city council. The city charter stated that if just a small percentage of those who had voted in the election signed a petition, then a recall vote had to be held. Very few people had voted in the last election so it was easy to obtain the required signatures. Belton had been established as a city and county seat in 1850. In all that time, no recall election had ever taken place, until we made it happen, in compliance with the city charter.

I did not expect the recall to be successful. Several of those on the city council were from families that had lived in Belton for over 100 years. The recall election was only to serve as a reminder to council members that they could be held accountable. On the day of the election, several cars beeped their horns in front of our house and passengers threw beer cans on our front lawn.

My children were embarrassed by my actions, as they had a direct impact on them at school and with their friends. My children would have no interest in attending class reunions later in life. They told me that their years at Belton High School were not the best years of their lives. Still, I do not regret doing what I considered to be my duty as a member of the Belton community.

In 1984 a joint military operation was scheduled in Honduras. The purpose of the operation was to deter the leader of Nicaragua, Daniel Ortega, from threatening bordering countries. The operation involved military forces from Panama, El Salvador, Honduras and the United States. They were to assemble in Honduras and conduct an airborne landing together, on the Honduran side of the border with Nicaragua. III Corps was tasked with providing the deputy operations officer for the joint task force.

I was instructed to recommend an officer to the corps commander. When I began looking for volunteers, there were none. I was advised to assign one of the lieutenant colonels on our staff. When he gave every excuse for not going, I recommended myself for the assignment. I was only a major and they wanted a lieutenant colonel, but after I reminded my supervisors that I was on the promotion list and wanted to go, they agreed to send me.

There were no weapons in Honduras for us; therefore I was directed to carry a .45 caliber weapon with me on a commercial plane. After taking my seat on the airplane, a flight attendant approached me and asked me softly, "Sir, are you carrying a weapon with you". After I replied "yes", she told me the pilot asked if he could keep the weapon in the cockpit. I turned over the weapon and loaded clips to the flight attendant.

I reported to MacDill Air Force Base, where planning for the operation was being conducted. The joint task force was being led by an Air Force brigadier general. The joint operations officer, J-3, was a short frail Army colonel who was very shy. My assignment was to serve as his deputy. We began planning and preparing to execute the plan to deter Nicaragua from invading its neighbors.

The general, the J-3 and I flew down to Honduras on a small Army plane on several occasions to meet with senior military and civilian leaders in order to coordinate the plan and its execution. The Honduran military officers felt threatened by the participation of the El Salvadoran Army. El Salvador had invaded Honduras in 1969 and killed many soldiers and civilians.

They reluctantly agreed to their participation and that of Panama and the United States. The joint military operation required all four countries to provide several hundred soldiers who were trained in airborne operations. All those participating would make an airborne landing on the border of Honduras and Nicaragua.

The joint task force established its headquarters in San Pedro Sula, Honduras. Soon after we arrived, I noticed that an Army unit assigned to provide security for the area had not been deployed. I visited the lieutenant colonel in charge and found that he had felt there was no need to deploy security.

We spoke outside in the pouring rain and the weather was one of his reasons for not deploying the soldiers in his command. I directed him to deploy his troops immediately and reminded him it was his mission. He immediately reminded me that he outranked me, being a lieutenant colonel whereas I was only a Major. I responded that I was representing the commander and those were his orders. He decided to comply with my directive and deployed his unit.

There were two Americans involved in the operation who caused some problems executing the mission. One was a Special Forces lieutenant colonel and the other a marine captain. The colonel was trained and qualified to jump out of airplanes, unlike myself who had never had a desire to jump out of a perfectly good airplane and had never been involved in an airborne operation. He was opposed to the entire operation and continually gave reasons why it should be cancelled. He claimed that the area we were to jump into had large stalks of grass and predicted that many jumpers would be injured.

The marine captain was more interested in the local ladies than preparing for the mission. On several occasions he became dehydrated in the hot jungle environment due to excessive alcohol consumption and entertaining the local ladies. He feared needles and would not allow medics to provide an IV for hydration. When I ordered him to comply he almost cried. He insisted I supervise the medic when he placed the IV in him and that the medic stick me with the needle after he received the IV to show me what it felt like. Neither he, nor the colonel, were assets to our team and should not have been assigned to the joint task force.

The United States provided a tent city to house the El Salvador and Honduran troops. The Honduran colonel refused to be housed in the same area as the El Salvadorans. He also insisted that each country's soldiers wear a different colored arm-band to distinguish them from one another. Despite repeated efforts, he would not agree to share the tent city with El Salvador.

We decided to let the Hondurans sleep in their own quarters and the El Salvadorans to use the tent city. Soldiers from the Panamanian Army were not due to enter the country until the day of the airborne jump. During the preparation phase, the Hondurans continually complained about the El Salvadoran Army, which did not help our efforts to show a united front to Nicaragua.

I decided to sponsor a party for leaders of the four countries. Many of those attending became intoxicated. While everyone was enjoying the moment, I began swapping their arm—bands, so that no one could tell who was from which country. Everyone found some humor in the event and recognized that the arm-bands were not really necessary. The next day, the order went out to remove them.

I befriended a Honduran major. One night, he insisted that we go to dinner at a local restaurant. I was planning to go without my side arm, a .45 caliber pistol, but he told me to keep it. At the restaurant, we were being closely watched by a large group of civilians who appeared armed and unfriendly. I felt relieved that they knew we were armed. After dinner, we went to a nightclub where he insisted I dance with one of his female friends. I felt very awkward dancing in a nightclub with a weapon in a holster attached to my belt but life, I learned long ago, can be full of interesting experiences.

A week before the scheduled jump, the Honduran colonel informed us that he was going to cancel his country's participation because of the danger warnings given by the Special Forces colonel. I recommended that the general, the J-3, the Honduran colonel and I visit the area of the landing, to demonstrate to him that it was not dangerous. We flew there by helicopter and visited the site, which happened to be close to a home owned by the equivalent of the U.S. Attorney General. We were all invited there for lunch and a discussion of politics in Honduras.

After our visit, the Hondurans were still reluctant to participate in the operation. I took the colonel aside and informed him that the operation would go on with or without his country's participation. I also added that Honduras would look very weak to everyone, especially when the El Salvadorans were planning to make the jump. He finally agreed to participate in the airborne jump because he did not want his soldiers to appear weak.

It was decided that on the day of the scheduled airborne exercise, I would be the operations officer on the ground and would make the decision for all participants from the four countries to jump out of the airplanes. The general and the J-3 wanted to be in the planes when the operation was executed. About an hour before the scheduled time for the airborne jump, the Special Forces colonel called me on the radio and told me there was machine gun fire in the area.

Normally, this would be an event that would cancel a peacetime operation. However, I believed he was lying because he was always trying to have the operation cancelled. I did not inform the general of the report when he called for the okay to execute the jump. I gave the "all clear" and within minutes about two thousand soldiers were jumping out of the planes. It was an awesome sight, watching men under parachutes landing all around me. I had never observed an airborne operation and here I was one of the men in charge.

During the jump, only four soldiers received minor injuries, which I was told was normal in any airborne operation of this size. The Honduran colonel approached me after the jump and asked where the trucks were to take his soldiers back to San Pedro Sula. We had all assumed each country would make plans for its own transportation home after the operation.

The United States Army had not deployed any transportation assets except for the planes that deployed the airborne soldiers. I told him he would have to arrange his own transportation. He replied that he would need the U.S. to provide rations while he waited several days to arrange transportation. We reluctantly provided some assistance to the Hondurans, who clearly were not good at planning military operations. El Salvador, Panama and the U.S. had made plans for the return of their soldiers.

When the operation was completed, I was anxious to return home. Several officers, including the Marine captain, planned to stay in the capital and party for a week or two. I chose to be on the next flight back to MacDill and then to Texas. On my return to Texas, I continued my efforts to return to a troop assignment. A few months later, I was given my next assignment, which was to be the 2nd Armored Division Artillery Liaison Officer, an assignment normally given to a lieutenant colonel.

The Division Artillery Commander, Colonel Merchant was the same officer, who when he was a major, attempted to damage my career in 1973 because of my support of African Americans who were experiencing discrimination. Despite those past experiences, we worked well together. One of my duties was to supervise the officer responsible for training and compliance with procedures and rules governing the transcription of secret codes related to the use of nuclear weapons.

The job was demanding and stressful because any officer responsible for a mistake could be fired. When the responsible officer left, I assigned a female captain to perform those duties. She refused to accept the assignment. I conferred with the commander and asked permission to ask for her resignation. I wanted to give her two weeks to make a final decision, but he told me to give her only 24 hours. She decided to resign from the Army the following day in lieu of disciplinary action.

A few months after her departure, I received a phone call from a local police officer in Colorado. She had applied for a position on his force and he wanted to know more about her. I provided a very positive review of her performance without mentioning why she left the Army. However, when he told me that she said that she left the Army because she had been discriminated against for being a woman, I was forced to explain the real reason she resigned from the Army.

During this assignment, LTC Corn was the executive officer of the unit. He often played golf with Colonel Merchant and the S-3, operations officer of the unit, LTC Welch. He considered LTC Welch a close friend. When a new division artillery commander was announced, LTC Corn began communicating with him. The new commander was none other than Colonel Cisneros, who had saved my career back in 1973 at Fort Hood, Texas. Back in 1973, Colonel Merchant had been the executive officer of the battalion and Colonel Cisneros had been the Battalion S-3.

Prior to his arrival, the incoming commander notified LTC Corn that he wanted me to be assigned as the S-3, operations officer of the division artillery. LTC Corn ignored that request until the new commander arrived. Within a few days, I was assigned to the S-3 position, much to the disappointment of both LTC Corn and LTC Welch.

The S-3, operations officer job is a good position to have on your resume when being considered for command of a battalion. It is a career enhancing position and sought after by senior majors and junior lieutenant colonels who have aspirations of commanding and moving up in their careers. Up to this point in my career, I had experiences as a battalion S-3, battalion executive officer, and now division artillery S-3, which would help my selection to command a battalion in the future.

When LTC Corn left his position as executive officer to command a battalion in our organization, I was selected to replace him, which again furthered my chances of being selected for command. In November 1984, a few months after being assigned as the executive officer, I was promoted to lieutenant colonel. One of my duties as the executive officer was to directly supervise the commander of the division artillery battery headquarters. His unit happened to have a lot of incidents where soldiers were fist fighting.

On one occasion, when I was given a report of a fist fight involving a soldier named Richard Trupiano, I decided to make an example of him and directed an investigation to determine if he should be court-martialed. I selected a major in whom I had total confidence to conduct the investigation. Major Toops had served in my command as an executive officer when I commanded a battery at Fort Hood in 1974. I strongly believed that there was enough evidence for a court martial. However, Major Toops reported that the soldier was defending himself and had not initiated the fight. I dropped the charges.

The commander of the battery headquarters was a captain who was very popular and happened to be a close friend of LTC Corn. LTC Corn was a battalion commander in our organization and had selected the captain for command when he was the division artillery executive officer. One day I was informed by a soldier that the captain had attended a party with enlisted men in the organization and had smoked marijuana.

The Army had, and still has, a very strict policy on illegal drug use. The policy is that the use of drugs by soldiers will result in termination of your service in the military. I investigated the complaint and was able to obtain statements from other soldiers that it had happened. When confronted, the captain denied it. LTC Corn immediately defended him and said the other soldiers must be lying, and that even if it was true, he should just be given a verbal reprimand.

I had punished many enlisted men during my career for drug use and had them discharged from the Army. I was not about to make an exception for an officer. Colonel Cisneros, the commander, approved of my recommendation to relieve him of command immediately and proceed with a court martial. He decided to resign from the Army in lieu of our taking disciplinary action. LTC Corn was furious, and on many occasions, complained about me to Colonel Cisneros. Colonel Cisneros ignored his complaining and reminded LTC Corn that I had never once criticized him.

Our organization regularly participated in field maneuvers at Fort Hood. On some occasions, our entire command, approximately 2,600 men and women, were deployed at the same time, with the division, which had about 16,000 men assigned to it. On one occasion, we were deployed at the same time as the Martin Luther King holiday. I initiated and planned a special Sunday memorial service in the field for the event. It was a very moving ceremony. The African American soldiers deeply appreciated the command taking the time to honor Dr. King while they were deployed in the field on maneuvers. The chaplain (the religious leader in a military unit), gave a moving sermon that involved paying tribute to Dr. King and his teachings.

In the summer of 1985, our son graduated from high school. He applied for several colleges but was only accepted by Texas Tech, which is located in Lubbock, Texas. When I asked him where he would be going to college, he said he did not have a choice and would have to go to Texas Tech. I suggested that he could enroll in summer school at the college he really wanted to go to, the University of Texas at Austin. I had completed some research into admission requirements and learned that any high school graduate could enroll in summer school. If the student achieved a 2.4 average and completed 12 credit hours during the summer, he could remain at the university in a probationary status for one year. My son took my advice and successfully met all requirements to graduate from the University of Texas.

I was scheduled for reassignment in the summer of 1986. The Army had nominated me to be the chairman of the military science department at The University of Vermont.

These assignments require the university to appoint you as a professor and provide office space for you to manage the

ROTC program. Army policy required the university to accept the Army's nominee. The University of Vermont did not want to accept my nomination without an interview, so they arranged for me to travel to Vermont at their expense.

At the interview, the administration said they had previously had some bad experiences with the Pentagon's nominees. They wanted a lieutenant colonel that was in the combat arms and had combat experience. They also wanted someone with an exceptional education history. I met their qualifications and they accepted my nomination. The department had its own building, which had an outstanding view over the campus. My office was especially comfortable and had its own fireplace. The university informed me they would also find a job for me on campus after I completed my three year tour and retired. I looked at homes in the area and signed a contract to purchase an historical home in St Albans. Our plan was to complete the assignment and then retire in Vermont.

As we were preparing to move to Vermont, I was selected for command of a battalion in Germany. I had the option of turning it down but a command assignment is a goal every career officer aspires to and works for, in his or her career. We had a family discussion of our choices, even though we knew what the decision would be. Everyone in the family knew that selection for command was a high honor, especially for a high school dropout and victim of poverty. We were concerned about the fact that we would be several thousand miles away from our son who was in college. However, in the summer of 1986, he was doing exceptionally well in his studies and managing his life in Austin. We planned on him visiting us in Germany during the summers and at Christmas times.

The Army selects battalion commanders based on a review of eligible officers' personnel files by a committee of senior officers, including generals. Officers are not interviewed as is the custom of most employers. Eligible officers for battalion command are lieutenant colonels or majors who were selected for promotion to lieutenant colonels. Officers are considered based on their career specialty and how many vacancies are projected for command.

Approximately 3,000 eligible field artillery officers were considered for command for about 90 vacancies in the year that I was selected. As mentioned earlier, what aided my selection was my experience in key positions such as battalion S-3 and executive officer, division artillery S-3 and executive officer, two tours of duty in combat, and two tours of duty in a command position. Outstanding performance reports from those assignments and having an advanced degree were also helpful in being selected for battalion command in 1986.

I was selected to command the 2nd Battalion, 377th Field Artillery unit in Herzogenaurach, Germany: the same unit I had served in 1978. The battalion had about 600 women and men assigned to it. It was the only artillery unit in which females could serve. Female soldiers were not allowed to serve in field artillery units except for field artillery missile units. Normally, missile units are positioned 15 to 20 miles behind the front lines.

The battalion had five batteries, each commanded by an officer with the rank of captain. There were three batteries armed with mobile missile launchers and support vehicles. Two batteries provided logistical, communications, and other administrative support. The firing batteries each had two mobile launchers capable of launching a missile with either a nuclear or conventional warhead. The capability of the nuclear warhead to inflict damage was secret. Although it cannot be revealed here, suffice it to say, the nuclear warhead was capable of inflicting major damage and casualties.

Prior to taking command and during the summer of 1986, the Army scheduled a self-paced German language course for me to attend at the Presidio of Monterey, California for six weeks. I asked my son, who was in college, to visit me for the last week of the course. We used that time to travel around California. While in California, I purchased a sports car, which we used to drive back to Texas when the course was completed. We sold our home in Belton and packed for our new assignment. The Army transported our family car and some household items to Germany and we paid to have the sports car transported.

In 1986 the economy in the United States was in turmoil. There were massive foreclosures, and auctions were held to sell houses and condominiums. We wanted to establish a temporary home in Texas before we departed for Germany. The home would serve as a place our son could use during our absence and provide us a place to stay between assignments. In late spring 1986, we decided to purchase a two-bedroom, two-bathroom condominium in Houston. The auctioneer warned everyone not to bid on a property that had not been viewed. However, we knew the area where the condominium was located and we successfully bid on it sight unseen. We furnished the condominium and stayed there for a few weekends and for most of the summer in 1986.

Fort Hood, TX, November 1984. Promotion to Lieutenant Colonel, (left to right): Colonel Marc Cisneros, Author, Mrs. Kimball, Kathryn Kimball.

Belton, TX, 1985. Author's family: (From front, left to right) Mrs. Kimball (wife), Lieutenant Colonel Kimball (Author); and their children Kathryn (12) and James (18).

CHAPTER SEVEN

Commanding Soldiers and Nuclear Missiles in Germany (1986-1989)

Our family, as was our custom, took 30 days of vacation time and traveled to New Hampshire to visit family, prior to flying to Germany for our new assignment. Unfortunately, the cabin on Squam Lake had been sold and the new owners were not interested in renting it out, so we stayed in a hotel in New Hampshire. We also took a one-week vacation in Florida that summer and visited Disneyworld.

Our assignment to Germany was scheduled to begin on December 16th. The Army did not encourage anyone to report early because housing was limited. Because family housing was unavailable, I departed for Germany without my family and had to spend Christmas without them. They stayed at the condominium in Houston to wait for permission to join me.

Normally, a new commander takes over the living quarters of the outgoing commander. However, for some reason, the outgoing commander was given permission to remain in his quarters after turning command over to me. As a result, I had to stay in a small room above the officers' club. Despite persistently inquiring as to when housing would be available for my family, I was given no definite date. Two months after taking command, I was offered what I considered substandard housing and refused to accept it.

I was furious, and informed the Brigade Commander, Colonel Potter, that I would not allow homeless people to live in the quarters he had selected for my family. I was then offered similar quarters, which I accepted (after repairs) because it was the same apartment we were assigned to during our prior tour of duty in Germany from 1978-1982. About nine months after my family arrived, the former battalion commander was reassigned and we finally moved into the appropriate quarters.

Colonel Potter had previously commanded the same battalion at Herzo Base that I had been assigned to. Everyone referred to him as "Ping Pong Potter" because he was always running around yelling at subordinates. He felt no one could measure up to the standard he had set when he commanded the battalion. He constantly attempted to micro-manage me and second guess all my decisions.

The outgoing commander had constantly been belittled and harassed by Colonel Potter. The prior commander had even stopped taking vacations or going anywhere on weekends because Colonel Potter would reprimand him every time he returned, for not knowing what had happened on the base while he was gone. He almost had a nervous breakdown due to the persecution inflicted on him by Colonel Potter.

I enjoyed my free time and intended to travel almost every weekend on trips with my family. I began a practice of calling my executive officer daily while on a weekend trip or vacation. As a result, when Colonel Potter contacted me on my return, I was well prepared to resolve any questions or issues. Sometimes, I chose not to answer his calls when I was on the base. His calls were intended to harass and intimidate me.

Colonel Potter had a terrible temper and would often scream on the phone when we conversed. I was generally not in the mood to hear his rants and raves about trivial matters. On one occasion, he questioned whether I had earned the decorations on my dress uniform, probably because several high ranking soldiers were being examined in the media over wearing medals they did not earn.

Naturally, I was furious that he would question my integrity and responded with a letter to him that reflected my anger and assailed him for questioning me on the matter. Colonel Potter had access to my military records and could easily have checked them before confronting me.

I knew that he would be angry after reading my letter. I had traveled away from the base for the weekend. He made many attempts to contact me while I was away, however I ignored them all. I also refused to answer the first ten calls he made to my apartment. When I eventually answered he directed me to step outside of my apartment and meet him in the street, as his residence was across the street from our apartment. As soon as I stepped outside, he began yelling and screaming at me. His first statement to me was to admit that he had been drinking.

The confrontation was witnessed by several officers living in the neighborhood who observed how upset he was. Colonel Potter used to tell people that communicating with him was like talking on a radio. On a radio, you push a button to talk and let it go when you want to listen. When I tried to respond to him, he said he was in a "push-to-talk" mode and that I could only listen.

While he was yelling at me, his face turned red and he was visibly shaking. After he finished and gave me a chance to speak, my response was, "Colonel Potter, you are going to have a heart attack right here in the middle of the street if you don't calm down". Those words made him even angrier because I had turned the subject of the conversation to his behavior, not mine. He then walked away from me, totally frustrated.

Colonel Potter became more hostile towards me as each day passed. I approached the brigade executive officer and asked him to schedule time at the end of the day so that Colonel Potter and I could talk about our differences and resolve to work better together. Colonel Potter refused my request.

A few months after taking command, our battalion received a new designation and unit number. We were to become the 2nd Battalion, 12th Field Artillery. Other units also received new unit numbers. Colonel Potter had ordered that the new numbers, 2/12 Field Artillery, could not be placed on bumpers of vehicles until the weekend before the effective date of the change, which happened to be the Monday of a four day weekend.

My command had about 80 vehicles, and I estimated that changing the bumper markings would take at least two days, perhaps three. Colonel Potter's order would require all the soldiers in my command to work on Friday, which was a holiday, and Saturday, ruining everybody's four-day weekend. As I mentioned earlier, I am a firm believer that if you take care of your soldiers, they will take care of you. I decided to ignore his order and directed my soldiers to start changing the bumper markings a few days early. The other units in his command decided to comply with his order and worked their soldiers on the four-day weekend.

Colonel Potter did not hear about my decision until after the vehicle bumpers were all changed. He ordered the guards at the entrance gate to the base to refuse to allow my vehicles to exit or enter the base. This was a major problem as our vehicles needed to leave the base daily to pick up food and vehicle parts, transport soldiers to medical or personal appointments, and conduct many other essential activities. I decided to give an order to the soldiers to cover up the vehicle bumpers with paper marked with the old unit designation when they had to leave the base. Technically, this complied with his order, so the gate guard allowed our vehicles through.

Colonel Potter ordered me to his office where he reprimanded me for not following his orders. He said to me in a very angry voice, "You don't follow my orders. How do I know you will follow my orders in combat?" I responded that our nuclear missile battalion was the number one target for the enemy. It was important that our movements and decisions were unpredictable; otherwise they could easily destroy us. I told him that if they don't know whose orders I will obey, the enemy will be confused too.

I am certain that it was at this point that Colonel Potter decided that one of his commanders was impossible to harass or intimidate. The soldiers in my battalion and their families enjoyed the four-day weekend, which annoyed the soldiers in the other units. In my opinion, Colonel Potter's order to have soldiers work on a four-day weekend was illogical and unfair. I had decided in the Vietnam War never to follow illogical or unfair orders that would result in harm to other soldiers.

One of my first challenges, besides dealing with the overbearing and micro-managing brigade commander, was to solve a problem that had a severe impact on our combat readiness. Our ability to communicate and receive orders to launch nuclear missiles against an enemy force depended on communication systems that were mounted on trucks.

Those vehicles were the only means for us to receive critical information and orders to launch nuclear missiles from headquarters. But when we deployed to the field for field exercises, several communication vehicles could not deploy because the soldiers responsible, who were mostly single women, were pregnant. As time went by, more female soldiers became pregnant, resulting in their non-deployment, thereby threatening our ability to perform our combat mission.

I believed that the women in the organization, about 35 enlisted and 5 officers, almost all of them single, did not understand birth control or refused to practice it, therefore, I made a command decision to educate them. I consulted with the five female officers about my plan and they all approved. When I informed Colonel Potter of my plan to have the base doctor, a female captain, give a class on birth control to all the women, he asked why the men would not receive the same class. My response was that they were not the soldiers getting pregnant and threatening our combat readiness. However, in hindsight and to be fair, I should have given them a similar type of class.

On the day the class was scheduled, I assembled all the female officers, female soldiers and the base doctor in the base theater. The doctor understood the importance of the issue. I explained to the female soldiers how our combat readiness and mission were being threatened by the increase in pregnancies in our battalion; how important their job was to the war time mission of the battalion; and that unplanned pregnancies could be avoided with the proper use of birth control techniques. After my brief remarks, I introduced the doctor and left the theater, because I felt the female soldiers would be uncomfortable with a man in the audience when birth control was being discussed. My solution to the problem of unwanted pregnancies worked. In the following 12 months, there were no reported pregnancies among the single female soldiers.

When my tour of command duty began, only enlisted female soldiers were allowed to serve in missile units. Soon after I took command, female officers were permitted to serve in our battalion. One of the first officers to report was a Captain Gifford, a member of the first class of female officers who graduated from West Point. She was smart, dedicated and qualified to serve as a Battery Commander.

After a few months serving in my S-3 (operations) section, I moved her into a command position. She became the first female commander of a firing battery in the Army and made every effort to impress the brigade commander. Captain Gifford did not approve of my command style and soon began complaining privately to Colonel Potter and providing him with information that he used to further his attempts to intimidate me. I became very disappointed in her disloyalty but resolved to accept it.

Another female officer was assigned to my S-2 section, which is the staff member responsible for security and intelligence. She desperately wanted to be selected for command of a battery. One day she asked for a meeting with me to discuss her future in the unit. As a captain, she held the rank that was authorized for a unit command.

She pointedly asked me about her chances of being selected for command, because she and her husband wanted to make a decision about becoming pregnant. If she had a chance of being selected for command, she did not want to become pregnant and be unable to deploy with a unit she commanded. I told her that she was asking me a question that would require me to decide when she would become a mother. Although she was an outstanding officer, I did not feel she was ready to command a unit at the time she met with me. I explained that I felt she was qualified, but that she needed a little more experience and suggested she should not put off motherhood. It felt awkward being in a position to impact a decision on when a life would begin for another person.

There were many personnel issues that I had to deal with regarding officers and enlisted soldiers in the battalion. In the Army, there was a lengthy process to discharge an officer from the military for inefficiency. Army regulations require the Pentagon to approve the discharge of an officer unless he or she committed a serious crime and was sentenced in a court martial. However, there was another exception, which according to my information, was never used in Germany until I used it. The exception was that if a new officer was incompetent or performed poorly, he or she could be discharged upon recommendation of the battalion commander. I used this exception to remove a second lieutenant from my command and from the U.S. Army.

The young lieutenant under my command was well liked by the other officers but not the men under his direct command. He was assigned to one of the firing batteries where he performed poorly. His unit commander (a captain) and I had both counseled the young lieutenant on a regular basis but counseling appeared to have no effect on the performance of his duties. I researched Army regulations and found that I had the authority to not only remove him from my unit and the U.S. Army but to revoke his commission as an officer. I met with him and gave him a final warning regarding his conduct and informed him of my authority to discharge him from the Army.

A few weeks after that meeting, we deployed to the field for three weeks of field maneuvers. These maneuvers involved living outdoors seven days a week, 24 hours a day. We deployed in the winter time, when it was cold and often snowing. Soldiers are provided special clothes to protect them in cold weather. During these exercises, the lieutenant continually got his unit lost, requiring his commander and me to search for his whereabouts. One day I visited his platoon to discuss his lack of map-reading skills after learning he had again become lost.

As I visited with the soldiers in his unit, I discovered a soldier without a field jacket and asked him where it was. He said the lieutenant was wearing it. I learned that he had deployed to the field without his winter clothes, toilet articles, towel or sleeping bag. He borrowed all of those items from his men, leaving them unequipped for the adverse weather conditions because of his own lack of preparation.

Upon my return to the base, I immediately submitted paperwork to revoke his commission and discharge him from the Army. The lieutenant went to all five battery commanders and asked them to speak to me on his behalf. As mentioned, the lieutenant was popular with the other officers and he used that to attempt to stop my actions. Four of the five commanders asked for a meeting with me to discuss my actions regarding the lieutenant. The lieutenant's commander, who was most familiar with the lieutenant, was the only commander who did not ask to meet with me. Normally, I do not reveal personal information to others but in the lieutenant's case, I felt I had no choice. After I explained the reasons, all the commanders agreed with my actions.

In the summer of 1987, we were scheduled to go to the island of Crete for the annual live fire exercise. Bennie, who had enlisted in the Army, was stationed at a nearby Army base. He had accumulated vacation time and wanted to go to the island of Crete on one of the available airplanes. When Colonel Potter heard that Bennie was being considered as one of the passengers, he immediately directed that Bennie not be allowed on any of the flights reserved for soldiers in our Battalion.

There was space for him to travel, but Colonel Potter enjoyed being in total control of my decisions and actions. Luckily, there were other flights to Crete from Germany that were not reserved for our battalion and Bennie flew on one of those flights. Colonel Potter was furious that he did not succeed in his efforts to thwart my plans. The day prior to departure, I met with Colonel Potter. When I asked him if there was anything we needed to discuss, he said there was nothing and wished us well. I later learned that the day after departure, Colonel Potter began investigating my leadership of the battalion by interviewing officers and senior NCOs. Evidently he was attempting to discover incriminating evidence he could use to relieve me of command.

The officers in my battalion reported to me that he had asked about everything that was going on in the unit. He gave them an opportunity to provide written complaints about me. To my knowledge, no one submitted a written complaint or provided any damaging information. When I returned from Crete, he acted as if his investigation of my command had never happened.

The live fire exercise in Crete went exceeding well. NATO members evaluated each of the firing battery's ability to launch a missile and found them all outstanding. As before, each of the three firing batteries rotated to Crete one week at a time, while I remained in Crete for the entire three weeks

After returning from Crete, I learned of my stepfather's death. I had only met him a few times and did not feel it was necessary to fly to the United States and be away from my command for ten days. Colonel Potter attempted to persuade me to leave Germany and to attend the funeral. I suspected he was looking for an opportunity to conduct another investigation of my command.

Every battalion has one NCO who acts as an executive assistant to the commander. He is the highest ranking enlisted man in the organization and his rank is command sergeant major. In my unit, he happened to be a soldier who had worked for Colonel Potter for many years and was close to him on a personal basis. He also happened to be an alcoholic. I encouraged my sergeant major to enter an alcohol treatment program but he felt he did not have a problem. Eventually, I had to order him into a program in Munich. I respected the sergeant major and believed he was very competent and loyal to me. It was one of the most difficult decisions I ever made while in command. His wife was very opposed to the treatment plan and met with Colonel Potter to argue against it.

The sergeant major appealed to Colonel Potter to revoke my order but Colonel Potter could not do that without jeopardizing his own Army career. In the Army, there is a chain of command. Colonel Potter technically was in command of the entire brigade of some 3,000 men and women. However, traditionally, he commands me and not the men and women in my command. He could give me orders, but, as a tradition, does not give direct orders to the soldiers under my command. The chain of command required him to go through me on all matters involving the soldiers in my command.

In the fall of 1987, a new commander, Colonel Vernon, replaced Colonel Potter whose two-year tour of command duty was completed. Colonel Vernon was obese, unable to run, a chain-smoker and appeared to be an alcoholic. The Army required physical training of all soldiers every day. I led the 600 plus soldiers in my command every weekday in physical training, which included a five mile run. Colonel Potter had almost always made an appearance at the 6:00 am formation but did not participate in actual physical training. Colonel Vernon rarely even bothered to show up for physical training at all while he was the brigade commander. At social events he drank and smoked excessively. In the evenings he often sat in his backyard with the officers who were his smoking and drinking buddies. I became very disillusioned with the Army's selection of its brigade level commanders and started thinking that it may be time for my Army career to come to an end.

Colonel Vernon had been a career staff officer who had very little experience in combat operations. He had experienced almost no involvement with the activities in any of the battalions he had commanded. His interactions with me indicated that he had been briefed by Colonel Potter on his objections to my leadership style.

In the summer of 1988, I contracted an infection as a result of dental surgery in Crete. I was not able to reduce a 104 °F temperature in spite of our unit doctor providing me various treatments. The doctor advised me to return immediately to Germany and enter a hospital for treatment. In spite of my illness, I made every attempt to perform my duties. When one unit was arriving from Germany, I went to the airport to greet it. At the airport, I could barely stand up and realized that I needed to follow the doctor's advice and return to Germany.

Reluctantly, I returned to Germany a week earlier than scheduled. I was immediately admitted to the hospital. The infection had caused my mouth to lock up. I was unable to open my mouth and continued to run a high fever. The doctors at the hospital informed my wife that if my body did not respond to the antibiotics, I would not survive the infection.

Colonel Vernon, as is customary in the military, should have visited me in the hospital. Instead, he sent one of the unit's medical officers to the hospital to inquire into my medical situation. Colonel Vernon was probably wishing that he would have the opportunity to replace me. After four days in the hospital, I was able to open my mouth slightly and realized that the antibiotics must be working. I was released from the hospital eight days after being admitted.

My command tour was scheduled to end in December 1988. I had given some thought to retiring because of my experiences working for incompetent superiors, who would have been responsible for many casualties if we went into combat. However, my primary concern was being forced to be separated from our children, which would be necessary if we continued to serve in the Army. In December 1988, I would turn 44 years old. I felt that if I wanted to begin a new career, I needed to begin it soon and not in ten years, which is the time the Army expected me to serve after command. The human resources department in the Pentagon contacted me and indicated I would be assigned to the Pentagon after completing my tour of duty. Lieutenant Colonels who successfully complete their command have about a 99 percent chance of being promoted to colonel and then given tenure, a guarantee of employment, for 30 years.

I received a second call from the Pentagon and was informed that I had been selected by the commander over all of the U.S. European forces to be a deputy operations officer at its headquarters in Heidelberg, Germany. Vyone and I had previously visited Heidelberg but went again to visit the city, since we would potentially be living there for four years. The Army policy was that if I accepted the assignment, I would have to stay in Germany for four more years. I would not be able to apply for retirement even though I was eligible to retire. Vyone enjoyed our visit to Heidelberg and was very excited at the thought of living there.

Our main concern was that we would be separated from our two children for four years. Kathryn was only two years away from graduating from high school, which meant she would be returning to the U.S. to attend college. Jim had already been separated from us for two years. If the Army had kept their original plan to assign me to Washington D.C. after my command tour ended, I think I would have reconsidered retirement. I recalled Colonel Vernon telling me that he had been in Germany for ten years straight and rarely saw his children. I did not want to be that kind of father to my children.

I made the decision to submit an application for retirement. Vyone was initially opposed to my retirement, but I had made a decision to go forward with my retirement. I did not want to go through the chain of command when I applied for retirement as I knew they would raise objections. In the Army, if you get the opportunity to command a battalion, they believe you owe them ten more years.

I traveled to the corps headquarters in Stuttgart, Germany and turned in my paperwork to a low-ranking clerk. I figured my decision to retire was between the U.S. Army in Washington D.C. and me. About a month after I submitted my application, I learned that a human resources officer had informed my commanding general of my retirement plans.

The next day, Colonel Vernon asked me to meet him in his office. He told me there had to be a mistake. He said he had been asked by the general if I was planning to retire. He informed me that he had replied "no" because he was not aware that I had submitted my application to retire, and had never even discussed the subject with me.

He reprimanded me for submitting the application without going through him. He said I had made a poor decision. He said the general was very upset. Colonel Vernon wanted me to think about it and call him in the morning. He said when I called him, he would have all the paperwork destroyed and he would never mention to anyone that I had planned to retire. His last words were, "we will forget this ever happened". I did not call Colonel

Vernon in the morning; I had made my decision. My decision to retire and return to Houston to complete my studies for a doctoral degree was final.

On the morning of December 16, 1988, the formal change of command ceremony was held in the gym because of a light snow fall. In addition to my family, several friends who I had known for more than 20 years including Richard Trupiano and Robert Ulin attended. After the ceremony, we departed Herzo Base for the last time and drove to the airport in Frankfurt.

Our flight to the U.S. was uneventful and not as emotional as our previous departure from Germany. In a lot of ways I felt relieved. I no longer faced the responsibilities of being deployed anywhere in the world as a soldier, being in harm's way and being separated from my family. I had served a total of 27 years, active and reserve, with the Army, and felt like I had completed my service in the Armed Services of our nation. However, even when you retire, you are not completely free from having to serve again in the Armed Forces. Retirement in the Army is often considered reduced pay for reduced services, since officially I was obligated as a retired soldier to return to active duty in the event of a national emergency, up until the age of 65.

We enjoyed a wonderful Christmas in 1988 as a family, with our son and daughter at our condominium in Houston. I had accrued over 60 days of vacation time and took that time to spend with family and to register and begin studies at the University of Houston. I registered for classes that began in January 1989, and officially retired from the Army on February 28, 1989.

V Corps, Germany, December 1988. Lieutenant Colonel Kimball, Commander, 1st Battalion, 12th Field Artillery with Missile Launcher and German soldiers in the background.

CHAPTER EIGHT

Schools need Principals with Principles (1989-2000)

I learned early on that living life often requires overcoming obstacles. The obstacles are always present, regardless of your age. In spite of registering for doctoral courses, I had not been readmitted into the doctoral degree program. The Chairman of the Educational Leadership Department at the University of Houston had not approved my repeated requests to be readmitted into the program.

I was very concerned, because if I was not accepted into the program, I would not be able to complete a goal in life that I had set many years earlier. One of the professors on the staff, Dr. Attanasi, who was very young for an assistant professor, offered to help me obtain readmission and advocated for me with the chairman. Finally, as the 1989 spring semester came to an end, I was officially accepted into the doctoral degree program.

While I was attending the University of Houston as a student, our daughter Kathryn began her 11th grade at a high school in the Houston area. The school had over 3,000 students, and within a block of it, there was another high school with over 3,000 students. She did not like attending the overcrowded, urban school. Vyone did not enjoy living in a big city. They both wanted to return to Belton. A few months after our return to

Texas, we traveled to Belton to attend the funeral of a childhood friend of Kathryn's.

Her friend, unknown to her parents, had secretly left the house late at night to see her boyfriend. They had an auto accident and were both killed. Prior to leaving for the funeral, a former neighbor who lived in Belton had called and asked me to look at an historic house when we visited the area. He was trying to find a buyer who would save the historic house from its rapid deterioration due to neglect and lack of maintenance.

The three-story historic home was one of the oldest houses in Texas. It was constructed around 1875 and was built with locally-quarried limestone. The home was owned in the late 1800's by a religious sect of mostly women, called the Sanctificationist, involved in a religion that inspired women to leave abusive husbands, join communal living, and run commercial enterprises. We were aware of the house and its history when we lived in Belton in the early 1980's. When viewed from the street the house looked very small, hidden behind the trees. After a tour of the house, I was impressed with its size and recognized the challenges that would be faced by anyone attempting its restoration.

After the funeral, Vyone and I made several trips to view the house and the Belton vicinity. When we questioned a local bank about a possible loan, they said they could not grant a loan due to the condition of the house. When a bank officer came to view the house, we were not able to enter the front door because it was too dangerous to walk on the porch with its rotted floor boards. I informed Vyone and Kathryn that purchasing the house was not possible. The house had been for sale for over five years and no one had shown any interest in buying it because of its poor condition. The owner was a single man who lived like a hermit and slept on the basement floor.

I secretly began negotiating with the owner without informing Vyone or Kathryn. They both desperately wanted the house and wanted to relocate to Belton. However, they had given up on the idea after I had told them it was not going to happen. One day in early August 1989, I received a call in Houston from the owner's agent and was informed that the owner had agreed to our offer as long as we would agree to close within 30 days. When I shared the news with Vyone and Kathryn they were elated and could not wait to leave Houston. There were a few problems at closing that threatened the deal, but eventually they were worked out. Immediately after the closing, Vyone and I went to the house and began painting the interior. There was no time to waste. We moved in early August and arranged to have all our furniture and belongings moved to the Belton house.

In August 1989, it had been two years since we had seen our belongings that had been placed in storage when we departed for Germany in 1986. It was like Christmas, opening boxes and placing the forgotten items somewhere in the large house. In the first few months, we focused on the outside of the house. Although the house included over two acres, there was no usable yard because the entire property was overgrown with trees and shrubs. As a family, we set to work cutting down trees and shrubs. We arranged to have approximately 25 truckloads of brush and dead wood hauled away so that we could have a front and back yard.

On Thanksgiving Day of 1989, we received a call late in the evening from Vyone's brother Larry who was living in Chicago. His partner Dale, who we considered a member of our family, had passed away from AIDS. We knew he had been ill and was fighting the disease. Unfortunately, many of the drugs that are available today that help people with HIV live a normal life were not available in 1989. It was a very sad occasion for us and for others who had learned to love and appreciate him.

There were many projects that needed to be completed in the house and we worked on them every day until I had to return to my classes at the University of Houston. After returning to classes, I commuted every weekend to Belton to work on the house. Most of the major projects (including installing 45 storm windows, painting, adding wallpaper, air conditioning and heating), were completed by the summer of 1990. That summer, our daughter Kathryn graduated from high school and decided to pursue a degree at Texas State University-San Marcos. Our son Jim also graduated that summer from the

University of Texas at Austin and obtained an engineering job with a company called Ford Aerospace, in Houston.

In the fall of 1990, our daughter and I were both in college. While she was studying for a degree for a future career, I was studying to obtain a doctorate for my second career. I completed my studies and received a doctorate in August 1991. I chose not to attend graduation ceremonies when receiving a bachelor's degree from California Polytechnic State University, a Master of Arts degree from the University of Oklahoma and a doctorate from the University of Houston.

My personal view of higher education is that if I decide to pursue it, then it's something I want to do. I felt that when I finished a degree program, I did not have to be rewarded with public recognition of my achievement. Achieving a higher education has its own rewards. Although we encouraged our children to go to college and graduate, it would not have made much difference to us if they chose not to. Our only desire for them was that they be happy in whatever life they chose to live. However, we were very proud to attend our children's graduations. It gave us a sense of success as parents and an opportunity to rejoice in our children's achievements. When my daughter graduated from her ROTC program in 1995 and became an Army Officer, I had the honor (as a retired officer in the United States Army) to render her the oath of office.

Upon completing the requirements for my doctorate in 1991, I decided to enroll in an alternative program for obtaining credentials to teach in public schools. I had difficulty entering the program because of my age, my desire to teach only at high school level, and the fact that I had a doctorate. The selectors for the program felt that I would not stay in teaching because I was overqualified. The program only had openings for elementary level teachers. At first, I was not selected for the program but a longtime friend, Cashin Clay, who knew the secretary to the person who selected candidates, successfully advocated on my behalf.

The program required me to take two courses at the University of Houston-Downtown. I also had to attend a four-week summer session and agree to pay for the program. Because the program only had openings for elementary teachers, I would have to find my own teaching position in a high school.

During the course of the program, I learned that the director and deputy director were alleged to be recruiting foreign nationals for the program and accepting bribes from those who were willing to pay to get into the program. I wrote an anonymous letter to officials sharing this information. The next day, the director addressed us and told us that she had received the first hate mail in her life, which was my letter to the officials. The program was investigated and she and her deputy had their employment terminated. The director sued the district, successfully proving that they did not have sufficient evidence to terminate her employment.

I began applying for a teaching position in Houston. I wanted to eventually become an administrator in a public school, but I knew that an applicant for that position had to (and should) have teaching experience. I had completed an application earlier in the year for a teaching position in the Houston Independent School District (HISD). However, when I had not received any offer of a teaching position, I decided to market myself.

I sent my resume to every middle and high school in the HISD. I received only one response and it happened to come in the form of a phone call on a Sunday. The caller was the principal of Lee High School. He asked me to meet him the next day for an interview to teach History and English. I was certified to teach History but not English. After the interview, I was offered a full time teaching position.

Lee High School is located in an area of Houston that has a very large immigrant population. In the 1960's, the student body was almost all white. When I began teaching, only six percent of the students were white. When classes began in the fall of 1991, almost none of the (approximately 45) students assigned to my 9th grade class could speak English. Also, there were various gangs in competition with each other. On several occasions I had to direct the students to lie down on the floor while gang members drove by, firing guns at the building. However, that was the least of my problems. I did not speak Spanish, which most of my students spoke. Each day I had a room full of students who had no idea what I was talking about.

I used very basic English and spoke slowly. My students were learning English in special classes for students with limited English proficiency. After a few months, they began to understand some of what I was teaching. I learned that many of my students were skipping other classes but were not skipping my classes. I believe it was because I made the learning material more relevant to the students and they felt that I really cared about them as individuals.

When I had to teach the differences between "the big stick" and "dollar diplomacy" political policies in the early 1900's, I walked around the room carrying a baseball bat in a threatening manner. After talking about the big stick policy of President T. Roosevelt, I exchanged the bat for 100 $1 bills to explain dollar diplomacy. I had the attention of every student in the class and had no doubt they understood those two very different political policies.

My students, like most 9th grade students, did not understand money management. Although it was not part of the History or English curricula, I planned a class to teach them about money. I had seven students sit at a long table. In front of each student was a sign that represented various household bills most people have to pay such as rent, electricity, food, car payments, car insurance, and gas for a car, and clothing. I then selected another student to approach the table and provided him with 100 $1 bills, which represented money they were paid at the end of a work week.

As the student went down the line, he or she had to pay bills. Before the student arrived at the end of the line, he or she had run out of money. This exercise helped the students understand the purpose of money and their financial responsibilities. They also recognized that I wanted to help them succeed in life. One of my students warned me that I should never bring that much money to class because there are some students who would kill for it.

Security officers working at the school were not armed with guns when I began teaching at Lee. However, within a year, the policy was changed. I believed at the time and continue to believe, that security officers should not openly carry guns as it gives students the impression that a school is a hostile environment, which impacts the learning environment.

While teaching at Lee High School, I began taking classes to be certified as a principal or vice principal in Texas. After I completed certification, I applied for a school administrator position in Houston. I was offered an administrator position in the central office of the HISD. However, I preferred to work at the campus level. I learned of an opening close to our home in Belton, Texas, and applied. I went to Killeen, Texas, and interviewed for an assistant principal position for either a middle school or a high school.

I was offered a position as vice principal at Eastern Hills Middle School in Harker Heights, Texas, and I accepted. I moved back into our home in Belton and began a career as an administrator in public education. When I was studying to be certified as an administrator, I had decided there were two policies I would implement as a school administrator. One, I would serve as a teacher for an entire day, five days a year, to be reminded of what teachers do on a daily basis. Secondly, I would request that teachers evaluate me twice each year, using a questionnaire that I prepared for them. I practiced this policy at every one of the seven schools I served at as an administrator. No other administrator at any of the seven schools ever elected to teach for a day or be evaluated. I initiated my personal policies for the first time at Eastern Hills and found the results very rewarding and helpful.

Although Eastern Hills Middle School was a predominantly white school, it was also a breeding ground for gangs. Most of the fathers of the students were serving in the Army at Fort Hood, which is the largest Army base in the United States. I spent many hours advising students to avoid gang fights at school, and outside of school. In Houston schools, there were gangs, but for the most part, they kept their gang activities off campus. (By avoiding being suspended or expelled, they could continue to sell drugs on campus.)

However, in Killeen, gangs of young teenagers would plot to have gang fights on campus. I found that the superintendent of the school district was in denial about the gang problem. I learned that parents, who had been gang members as youths, were supporting gangs by hosting meetings at their homes. Oftentimes, I found myself alone, outside, during lunch breaks trying to keep gangs from fighting each other. Unlike in the HISD, middle schools in Killeen did not have security officers on campus.

One of the parents, who was a sergeant in the Army and who sponsored gang meetings at his house, complained when I reported that his son was a gang leader. When we met with the father, he argued that his son was being harassed and being threatened by other students. However, the fact was that his son was instigating gang fights on campus and leading the fights when they began. On one occasion, the father physically threatened me on the campus, and we believed he had a gun in his possession. When we successfully removed the student from the campus, gang activity was reduced.

The Killeen school districts had their own police force which visited the campus often. On one occasion, I noticed an adult male walking in the hall, armed with a sidearm. I immediately asked him to identify himself and he responded that he was a police officer. I complained to the Chief of Police that his police officers were not wearing their police badges when they entered our buildings. I requested that he direct them to wear badges so that we could recognize them. The Chief of Police questioned the police officer who then falsely stated that he had been wearing a badge.

Another incident would lead to the deterioration of my working relationship with the police. At the football games, I would often ask the police to patrol the area individually, instead of milling around in groups of three. On one occasion, we received a threat that a gun would be used to shoot a rival gang member. We decided to search all those who attended the game with a portable metal detector. To discredit me, the police officers on duty falsely reported that I searched only Hispanic students. I became increasingly disappointed by the lack of support shown by the superintendent and the district's police officers in dealing with the gang problems.

While I was working at Eastern Hills Middle School, our daughter met Frank Elkins, who she married on December 31, 1994. He was also a student at the University of Texas-San Marcos, and like Kathryn, was enrolled in the Army ROTC program. A few months later she graduated with a Bachelor of Science degree and obtained a science teaching position at a junior high school in Manor, Texas, a few miles from Austin. Our son Jim, and his wife, Debbie, had their first child (our first grandchild) on July 31, 1995, in Pearland, Texas. They named her Nicole Elizabeth Kimball.

I did not feel effective as a school administrator in Killeen because of a lack of support from the district. In 1996 I decided to apply for a vice principal position in Houston. I resigned from Eastern Hills Middle School and accepted a position at Pershing Middle School in the HISD. I had previously been interviewed at Lee High School for the same position. At Lee, the principal, who happened to be white, informed me that I was his choice for the position. However, because he was required to have racial diversity, he had selected an African American lady for the position. I had no problem with his decision because public schools should make every effort to select administrators who are representing the ethnicity of their students. At Lee High School, only six percent of the students were white.

I believe that I was selected over 20 other candidates who were interviewed for the position at Pershing Middle School partly because I was a white male and had experience as a teacher and administrator. The 6th grade and 8th grade principals were both African American and female. The school needed a white male for diversity. The student body at Pershing was 35 percent white. While Lee High School was located in a very poor immigrant neighborhood, Pershing Middle School was located in one of the most affluent areas in Houston.

Since I would be working in Houston, we decided to purchase a house in Houston and sell our condominium. The buyer offered to purchase the entire contents of the condominium, including all the furniture, televisions, dishes, pots, pans, and wall art. I agreed to his offer and left the condominium taking only my personal items. His intention was to house his mistress at the condominium. His wife, I learned, knew nothing of this purchase. In Texas, the law allows a married man to purchase property under his own name but when he sells; his wife has to be involved. In 1996 we purchased a house in West Houston in a low socio-economic neighborhood. We also bought the house next door as an investment and rented it to friends. Vyone and I took turns commuting on weekends to be with each other. She was not ready to move to Houston or sell our Belton house.

In 1996 Pershing Middle School was located in a very old building, which would eventually be replaced in 2007. The teachers were very effective and the students were well-behaved. There were no gang problems and fights between students were very rare. For the most part, my job consisted of counseling teachers, students and parents. Unfortunately, the three female counselors on the staff preferred not to counsel students, especially those who had emotional problems. They resented me sending students to them for further counseling, especially when they were emotionally upset and crying. They specifically told me not to send them a student who was crying.

The coaches at the school also became my adversaries. The HISD had decided on a policy that prohibited the use of corporal punishment. The policy provided for termination of employment of those who did not comply. At Pershing, there was no need for such a policy because students were well-behaved. However, some parents had made arrangements with the coaches at the school to use corporal punishment on their children for a variety of reasons, some not even related to school activities. When I learned of this special arrangement with the coaches, I wrote a letter to each coach that stated I would move to terminate the employment of any teacher or coach who inflicted corporal punishment for any reason. The coaches understood that the district policy would be enforced and the special arrangements with the parents ceased.

Students were sent to one of the vice principals for minor discipline problems each day. It was the responsibility of the administrator to investigate the discipline issue and determine punishment or simply counsel the student or students involved. On one occasion, the 6th grade principal (who was black) asked me to handle the discipline of three white students in her grade, because their parents felt that she was prejudiced.

The three white students had harassed a black student by playing a game, which treated the black student like a slave. The harassment included derogatory statements and lightly striking the student with a rope to simulate the beating of a slave. After conducting my own investigation, I determined that the punishment assigned by the 6th grade principal was not harsh enough. I informed the parents of the white students that I would have suspended the students for three days instead of just one day, and I would also have insisted on counseling.

Racial issues came up frequently at Pershing Middle School, even among the faculty and staff. The 8th grade principal happened to have very dark black skin while the 6th grade principal had very light black skin. On an almost daily basis, the 8th grade principal referred to the 6th grade principal as being my "sister", by which she meant that the 6th grade principal's skin color was closer to mine, than that of the 8th grade principal. This was intended as an insult to her for being "mixed" and questioning her ethnicity. Some white parents requested in writing that their child, who was either in the 6th or 8th grade, be assigned to me, a 7th grade principal, for behavior issues. The principal often approved these requests, which I felt was counter-productive in terms of race relations on campus.

Another racial issue developed at the school with a very popular African American music teacher. She had received many letters from important political figures in the community commending the public performance of her choirs. However, when I visited her classroom, I oftentimes found her to be absent. She often left her students unattended, which resulted in students misbehaving. In one incident, a 14-year-old female student had her bra ripped off by a male student. When I admonished the teacher in writing for the discipline problems in her classroom, she immediately filed a complaint with the teachers' union. The principal gave in to pressure from the teacher and the teachers' union and removed the letter from her record.

My relationship with the counselors and principal became strained as the year progressed. The counselors did not like me sending students to them for counseling or schedule changes. I believed that sometimes student schedules needed to be changed because some behavioral problems were directly related to the student not being liked by the teacher, or vice versa. Often, I felt the student and teacher would best be served by changing the student's schedule. This solution created extra work for the counselors, and I had the distinct impression that they did not like doing their job. They often voiced negative opinions to the principal concerning my actions. At the same time, I worked to convince the principal to change some policies that would create a more positive environment at the school. He was receptive to some, but not all, of my recommendations.

At the end of my second year at Pershing, I was informed that I would be transferred to Welch Middle School and a vice principal there who the principal did not like would replace me. 95 percent of the students at Welch Middle School were black, as well as most of the teachers. The school was led by a very young and inexperienced white principal who was totally incompetent. I had a conflict with the principal on my first day and had requested a transfer within two days of my arrival at the school.

One of my first actions as assistant principal was to have a soiled couch in the teachers' break room removed, at the teachers' request. They informed me that the couch had a terrible odor and had many stains from being used by custodians at night. I immediately requested that the custodians remove the couch from the break room.

The principal, upon his return and upon first meeting me, reprimanded me for removing the couch and had it returned to the break room. I decided immediately, based on his authoritarian leadership style and limited management skills that I would not be able to work with him. On subsequent meetings with him, he rejected every request and recommendation I made that was aimed at improving the environment at the school.

He would not approve supply requests for copy paper, paper towels, soap, or toilet paper for the restrooms. He had obviously decided that he would disapprove any request that I made to him. Teachers, students and parents complained about the lack of supplies in the school. He refused to replace the computer mousses stolen by students. Since the computer teacher could not teach her class without functioning computers, many fights between students took place in her classroom.

I had to go into her classroom every day to resolve student fights or other behavioral problems. I pleaded with the principal to approve purchasing computer mousses, but to no avail. He believed that if he created a hostile environment for the computer teacher, she would retire or quit. He eventually succeeded because she decided to retire in the middle of that school year.

When the school's most incompetent teacher falsely claimed that she had been assaulted by a student, he approved a two-year leave of absence with full pay for her. When I provided evidence that she had not been assaulted, he rejected it and said he just wanted the teacher out of the school building because she had been complaining about him and he felt she was not an effective teacher.

A new teacher who taught the special education students was provided no additional assistance, in spite of having 30 special education students in her class. One of the few white students at the school, who happened to be a special education student, was constantly bullied in the cafeteria and in the hallways. His parents asked for a transfer and the principal refused to approve it. When the other vice principals and I met with the principal to discuss issues and concerns, they would never speak up. I was the only administrator, besides the principal, who spoke at the meetings. At each meeting, I addressed serious concerns and his only response was that he would look into it but he never did.

After a few weeks at the school, I began preparing a letter to the area superintendent with a list of the principal's poor management decisions and wrongdoings. I delivered the letters to the area superintendent's office every Friday after school.

The area superintendent, Dr. Kaye Stripling, who eventually became the district superintendent, discussed the letters with the principal. After reviewing the letters for about two months, she arranged a meeting with the principal and me.

At the meeting she engaged us in some role playing. She played myself and asked the principal what he should do about some of the complaints in my letter. His response was that I had no right to question anything he did as the principal. He was the principal and it was my duty to perform assigned tasks only. It was obvious that the principal was not going to change his attitude or address my concerns. Dr. Stripling had to have realized that he was closed-minded.

After this meeting, I continued to send letters every Friday to Dr. Stripling. The principal called me to his office and asked me when I would stop sending the letters. I responded that they would stop when he approved my transfer to another school. He decided to write a letter of reprimand to me for something that had no basis in fact. His letter was in retaliation for my letters to the area superintendent. I sent an email to Dr. Stripling and demanded the reprimand be withdrawn and it was.

I followed up with a letter to the District Superintendent, Dr. Rod Paige asking for his intervention. I attached all the previous letters to the area superintendent, letters to the principal and documentation providing evidence of mismanagement and wrongdoings of the principal. After 30 days I sent a letter to Dr. Paige requesting a response. He finally replied and stated that I should work with the principal and area superintendent to resolve my concerns.

After receiving this response, I sent the entire package and a cover letter asking for assistance to the board president at the HISD. He responded within 72 hours by letter, stating he would look into the matter. A few days later, Dr. Stripling informed me she wanted to visit with me at the school. At that meeting, she said she had discussed my concerns with Dr. Paige and the board president, and it had been decided that I would be transferred to another school.

She said she had discussed my transfer with Anne Patterson, West District Superintendent, who had agreed to assign me to a school in her area. I had met Anne Patterson earlier in the year when I interviewed for a vice principal position in her area. Unfortunately, the policy in most districts is to ignore valid concerns and wrongdoings by transferring the person who dares to address school problems to another school.

Around this time, our second and third grandchildren were born. Cameron Kimball was born on October 17, 1998 in Orlando, Florida where Jim and his family were then living, after being transferred by his employer. Our third grandchild was born to Kathryn and Frank on March 31, 1999. Jami Rae Elkins was born at Fort Hood at the same hospital where our daughter was born in 1972. We were fortunate to be at the hospital when she was delivered. We were taken to the room where she was cleaned up by a nurse after the delivery. Frank was in the Army at the time and was stationed at Fort Hood. Soon after Jami Rae was born, Frank and our daughter decided on a change of career path. He resigned from the Army as a captain, and they moved to Tulsa, Oklahoma, where he had been hired for a communications position with a large oil and gas corporation.

After my transfer from Welch Middle School, I decided to provide my letters to school leaders and documentation of mismanagement and wrongdoings at Welch Middle School to a local affiliate of CBS News. The television station aired a story on the problems at Welch and interviewed the young special education teacher who had resigned when she received no assistance from the principal. They also interviewed the young white special education student who was bullied by other students. Some teachers who were interviewed spoke of witnessing students having sex under the stairways and in classrooms, and other problems at the school. In spite of all the documentation and television coverage at the school, the principal was promoted to a very high level administrative position in the district. We had a saying in the Army: "those who screw up, move up"; and it appeared to be just as true in the civilian world.

In the middle of the academic year, I was assigned to Grady Elementary School, in an affluent area, close to the Galleria in Houston. The principal had instructions from Anne Patterson that I was to be assigned limited duties. I was not permitted to handle discipline issues or evaluate teachers which are the two primary responsibilities of a vice principal.

Basically, I was to monitor hallways between classes and supervise the cafeteria at lunch times. After a few months, the principal obtained permission for me to begin handling some discipline issues and some teacher evaluations. At the end of the year, the principal was asked by Anne Patterson if she wanted me to return the following academic year and she replied, "Yes".

At the beginning of the next academic year, I attended a three-day teacher workshop held before students returned to school. At the workshop, I decided to sit with the teachers rather than the other vice principal and principal. I thought that the teachers felt it was them against the administrators on the campus, and I wanted to change that image. The principal was offended that I sat with the teachers and not the leadership group. She called Anne Patterson and asked that I be transferred from her campus after the first day of training. I was directed to report to the area superintendent's office where I was to remain for a month without any duties.

After a month of sitting in an office and not having any duties, I was called into Anne Patterson's office and told that one of her high schools needed some temporary help because one of the assistant principals had to take emergency leave. I was to report to the principal and perform duties assigned to me by her. It was made very clear to me that this was a temporary assignment and I would be there for just a few weeks in the fall of 2000.

CHAPTER NINE

On becoming a Whistleblower (2000-2004)

Sharpstown High School is located in a poor immigrant neighborhood not too far from Lee High School. It too, had been predominantly white in the 1960's but now was predominantly Hispanic. The principal, Dr. Carol Wichmann, had retired from another school district, but was urged to return to work and accept the position at Sharpstown High School. She was a very gracious and attractive woman in her mid-sixties.

The principal and I quickly gained mutual respect for one another. Her leadership ability was outstanding and in my view she would have reached general officer rank, if she had chosen the military as a career. She was totally supportive of any recommendations I proposed relating to the management of the school and the actions I took. She often sided with me at meetings over the objections of the other five vice principals. At Sharpstown High School vice principals were referred to as "deans". After a few months, she asked the area superintendent, Anne Patterson to assign me as a dean at the school on a permanent basis. I was given all the duties normally assigned to a dean.

During this time, the HISD was changing many policies in the district. The most important policy change was to decentralize operations, which I believe was a grave management error. Under decentralization, each school was provided a budget and the principal was given the authority to decide on how to spend the funds. This policy change required a business manager position at each school.

Dr. Wichmann asked me to apply for a district training and certification course for business managers and become the school's business manager. I declined at first, but she was insistent, so I applied for and was accepted into the very competitive training course. The six month course would require me to leave the campus and train at the district. I began having second thoughts because of slated major construction projects at our school and the fact that I had no interest in being a student again.

When the time arrived for me to begin the business management course, I went to Dr. Wichmann and asked for her support in relieving me of the responsibility of participating in the business management course. I reminded her of the campus renovation project that was about to begin and that I needed to be on campus to supervise the renovations. She agreed, and I was not required to attend the business management program.

Our school had been approved and scheduled for renovation in 2001-2002. The amount approved for the renovation was $16M. I was assigned to manage the renovations. Normally, deans do not work over the entire summer. I was asked to work that summer and the next summer to supervise the renovations. During the summer of 2001, the school was completely gutted. The workmanship of the contractors was very poor. I sent many emails to the district complaining of the poor quality of the workmanship and materials used.

One of the foremen of the renovations team complained to me about my emails. He confronted me in a very threatening manner. He was about 6'7" and put his body within six inches of me. He told me in front of the other contractors that he was going to arrange for me to be fired soon. However, I had the total support of the principal and was not concerned with his threats. A few months later, the contractor was fired for corruption.

A few weeks before classes were due to begin for the 2001 fall semester the school was still not ready to open. The air conditioning system was not operational, desks had not been placed back in classrooms and computers were not set up in any of the classrooms. But because the staff worked long hours with the contractors, we were able to open on the first day of classes.

My emails to the district were frank and very critical of the district and contractors' roles in the renovations. The media decided to do a story on the waste of tax dollars involved in the renovations. An ABC affiliate specifically requested that I provide a tour of the campus and discuss the renovations. The reporter repeatedly asked me about my critical emails. I knew that if I had painted as bad a picture of the project on camera as I had in my emails, I would probably be transferred again.

I decided to be evasive when responding to his questions. In the newscast, I was shown in color at the beginning and when I became evasive, the color changed to black and white. I learned long ago that you have to decide which battles to fight and when to fall on your sword. This was not the day to do either. Events would soon lead me to a much larger and more important confrontation with the school district.

On September 11, 2001, we began receiving reports concerning the twin towers in New York. I advised the principal to go on the intercom system and share the news, and to advise students and teachers that we would keep them updated as to what was happening in New York. Parents began calling in to the school requesting to pick up their children and we began to arrange to have them ready. When parents asked what they should do, we advised them to allow their children to complete the school day.

I went into many classrooms and asked teachers to discuss the events with their students. The teachers told me they were not prepared to do that as they were not trained to be social workers. I found that response to be a poor excuse for being unwilling to help calm student fears. However, September 11, 2001 was not the time and place to debate this issue with teachers.

I officially became the business manager of the school in the fall of 2001. However, I insisted on continuing with duties normally given to a dean. I continued to evaluate teachers and handle discipline problems in addition to being the business manager. The principal told me on many occasions that finances were her weakness and insisted I handle everything dealing with funding. Many of the responsibilities she had in funding were turned over to me. She praised me frequently in front of other deans, staff and to the area superintendent. One day during a visit, Anne Patterson, told me she wished she could clone me.

After I completed my first year at Sharpstown High School, Kathryn and Frank had their second child (our fourth grandchild): Kori West Elkins. He was born on August 24, 2001 in Tulsa, Oklahoma. After his birth, each of our two children had one son and one daughter in their family. Our immediate family now included a total of ten.

At Sharpstown High School, I often walked the halls with the other deans to monitor behavior between classes. Some of the deans acted as bouncers. During these hall sweeps, they would confront students and tell them to go to the office and withdraw from school. They told them that they had too many discipline issues or were absent too often. These students, without questioning, would dutifully head to the registrars' office and withdraw from school. I began witnessing a trend of administrators ordering low-performing students to withdraw from our school.

One of my additional duties as a dean was to manage the issue and retrieval of textbooks. When a student withdrew from the campus for any reason, he or she had to obtain my signature after turning in their books. When they visited my office for a clearance on textbooks, I would ask them why they were leaving. Oftentimes, they told me that a dean had told them to withdraw from school.

In one case a student who had been directed to withdraw was only 15 years old and was classified as a special education student. I sent a very testy email to the principal explaining that students cannot be kicked out of school because of low performance and that it was illegal to force a 15-year-old student to quit school. She overruled the dean and allowed the student to remain in school. However, as soon as the student turned 16, the dean again ordered the special education student to withdraw from school. Fortunately, that dean's employment was terminated when a criminal background check indicated she had a criminal record that she had not disclosed when she was hired.

Sometimes, the deans referred students to "discipline alternative-education placements" (DAEPs), which involved sending the student to an "alternative school" set up for students who were deemed to have discipline or attendance problems. The alternative school was several miles away from our school and was managed by a private company called Community Education Partners (CEP). I visited the school on many occasions and talked to the students from our school. I found the school operated much like a prison and provided minimal educational services to students. It appeared to me to be a place where students were dumped in the hope that they would drop out of school.

Students were searched upon entering the campus. They were confined to one room all day except for a lunch period. Restrooms were located in the classroom and each had a light above the door to indicate if it was in use. Students were required to sit in front of a computer all day and complete academic work on a self-paced basis. The district was paying over $11,000 for each slot in this program, more than twice the amount provided to regular schools to educate students.

One of the major criticisms of the company's contract with school districts was the requirement that a district purchase slots for students. While school districts in Texas are paid for actual students in attendance, CEP requires payment for a set amount of slots. For example, the HISD paid approximately $11,000 for each of the 1,600 slots for students in school year 2010-2011. However, as of January 1, 2011, reports indicated that about 900 students were enrolled on any one day of the school year up to January 2011. The HISD appeared to be paying for approximately 700 students who were not enrolled in the company's schools at a cost of about $11,000 per student which amounted to millions of wasted tax-payer dollars.

Sending students to the alternative school was part of a growing trend at our school to remove low-performing students. There were good reasons for schools to remove low-performing students. Every school in Texas is given a rating based on students' collective academic achievement. A low rating for three consecutive years can result in the school being closed by the Texas Education Agency (TEA). Schools quickly learned that if you remove the low-performing students, ratings will improve. I soon learned that this was not just happening at our school. Some schools were intentionally keeping 9th grade students in the 9th grade for several years to prevent them taking part in tests given in the 10th grade that determined school ratings.

HISD administrators and school board members had noticed that some schools had achieved dramatic increases in their ratings and learned that they had accomplished it by keeping 9th graders from being promoted to the 10th grade. Some high schools were reported to be retaining over 50 percent of 9th graders in grade at the end of the school year. The district praised what some high schools were doing to increase their ratings. The school board eventually passed a policy that required that all 9th grade students in the district pass all classes before they could be promoted to the 10th grade.

As a result, tens of thousands of 9th graders were retained in the 9th grade. School ratings were based on the number of students who passed state examinations given in the 10th grade. The number who passed the test increased significantly because low performers were retained in the 9th grade. Many of those retained quit school. Statistical data clearly shows that students retained for one year in the 9th grade have a 50 percent chance of dropping out of school; students retained two years have a 75 percent chance of dropping out of school. Administrators and school board members had no sympathy for the dropouts. Some of them declared privately that those students would have dropped out regardless of being retained in grade.

The dropout rate is considered in school ratings so the district had to cover up the increasing dropout rate. In 1997 the state had threatened to withdraw the district's accreditation because its reported dropout rate was close to 25 percent. Dr.

Paige, the superintendent at the time, had to deal with the dropout rate quickly or lose the district's accreditation and the potential to become the next U.S. Secretary of Education. He and other administrators were able to accomplish that easily and by 2002 were reporting a dropout rate of only 1.7 percent. They accomplished this so called, "Texas Miracle" by using what were called "leaver codes", developed by the state to cover up the dropout rate.

Leaver codes were used by the state to explain why a student was no longer enrolled in school. Students assigned certain leaver codes were not considered dropouts. Basically, all a school had to do was to assign a leaver code that did not classify the student as a dropout. If a school did not assign the right leaver code and the dropout rate increased, a principal would be looking for a new job. Some of the leaver codes that exempted a student from being coded as a dropout included transfer to a private school, home school, charter school, or GED program, a return to the home country or a move out of state.

As a high school dropout, I was personally offended by what I was witnessing in the public school system in Texas. I began to become increasingly concerned about my role in this dishonest, immoral, and illegal policy, which dumped kids on to the streets just because they were low performers or had too many absences. My decision to become involved and make a difference would soon place me in a national debate on the dropout crisis and involve me in the campaign of the incumbent U.S. Presidential candidate who claimed to be the "education president".

In late 2002 President Bush began his campaign for a second term as the President of the United States. During his many campaign speeches he often referred to the "Texas Miracle" for which he claimed credit when he served as governor of the state of Texas. He claimed that he reduced the dropout rate, increased the graduation rate and raised the performance of students on academic tests. At that time, I was not paying much attention to this campaign issue, but his claims would soon bring national attention to Sharpstown High school and me.

After witnessing so many students dropping out of our school, I asked the principal for permission to conduct a study of dropouts. My proposal would require students to complete a survey as to why they were dropping out of school. On occasion, when I had time, I would interview them and assist them with the survey. However, most of the time, they just completed the survey and gave it to one of the clerks in my office. There was no doubt that students were dropping out because many of them had come to my office to obtain a textbook clearance and fill out the dropout survey.

In October 2002, the HISD was selected as the winner of the Broad prize for being the best school district in the nation. National recognition of the district increased the credibility of a presidential candidate who claimed that he was responsible for the Texas miracle. Soon after the award was accepted (Oct 28, 2002), the technology manager, Kenneth Cuadra, came to my desk to share a report he was going to submit to the district and state.

The report stated that our high school had zero dropouts. I asked him how we could possibly report zero dropouts when there were so many dropouts. He said it's what the principal wanted him to report and explained the leaver code system to me, which up until that moment, I knew nothing about. I soon learned that of 463 students who withdrew from Sharpstown High School that year, not one student was reported as a dropout. Leaver codes were falsified so that no dropouts were on record. It was apparent to me that the "books were being cooked" at our school and perhaps throughout the district.

On November 5, 2002, I sent two emails to the principal and, again on November 11, 2002, regarding the zero dropout report. In the email, I asked for a meeting to discuss the reported dropout rate. I wrote in the email, "We have no dropouts! Amazing! We go from 1000 freshman to less than 300 seniors with no dropouts". I also stated that the zero dropout report does not "reflect what we learned from our contact with parents of those students on the dropout list".

A few days later I happened to be in the principal's office on another matter. I asked her when we could meet to discuss my concerns about the zero dropout report. She told me that when she began the job as principal she was told by the area superintendent, Anne Patterson, that Sharpstown High School had a dropout problem and that it could be taken care of by doing the paperwork right, or something to that effect. The principal added that if anything went wrong, she would simply say she was told to do it by her supervisor, Anne Patterson.

Soon after I became aware that a false report had been submitted on dropouts, I had a long conversation with Houston Federation of Teachers (HFT) Representative Rosemary Covalt. She was in our building representing a teacher and was leaving when we began a conversation about the dropout crisis. She told me that minority organizations in Houston have been trying to address the dropout problem for over 20 years to no avail.

She said that without data to prove the district was making false reports, there was nothing else they could do and that she had given up on addressing the dropout crisis. I told her that I was not going to give up and that I accepted the challenge to make a difference and address the dropout crisis. I told her that I had evidence that Sharpstown High School was reporting zero dropouts when in fact it had many dropouts.

The next day, Rosemary asked if I would meet with State Representative Rick Noriega, HISD Board Member Esther Campos, and Rosemary to discuss my evidence. I agreed and at the meeting I provided evidence that a false report had been made by Sharpstown High School on dropouts. It was decided that Representative Noriega would call for an investigation by the TEA, I would work with the media, and that Esther would monitor events at the district.

Rosemary had informed her media contacts at Channel 11 (a CBS affiliate) of the zero dropout reports and told them that I was willing to meet with them. As a former military officer, I understand the chain of command. I understood that I should report the problem to the principal's supervisor. However, I had already been told that she was the one that directed the principal to fix the problem by fixing the paperwork. I already had experience with trying to bring wrongdoings at Welch Middle school to the area superintendent, the district superintendent and the HISD board president. I learned from that experience that if I tried to do that with the Sharpstown wrongdoings, it would only result in another transfer and no action would be taken to address the falsification of student data.

I was not the only person who was questioning the zero dropout report. Ms. Nolte of the Office of Compliance at the TEA sent an email to Dr. Wichmann on December 18, 2002. In it she wrote, "I find it very difficult to think that [at] a school with 74.7% of the students at risk that there would be no dropouts". The superintendent, Dr. Kaye Stripling, had hired an outside law firm, famous for defending criminals, to conduct an investigation into my allegations. In order to limit the damage to the district, she ordered that the investigation only investigate Sharpstown high school.

Dr. Stripling, who was not certified to be a superintendent, and knew the problem was district wide, had decided to control the damage. A report in the Houston Chronicle on June 18, 2003, reported that the "false or negligent record keeping is not isolated, but district wide". On September 14, 1994, Dr. Stripling, while serving as a Deputy Superintendent, was given a letter of reprimand by the HISD District Superintendent, Rod Paige, for mismanagement and falsifying a document. Seven years later she was promoted and signed a very lucrative contract (over $200,000 annually) to serve as the Superintendent of the district. In the contract signed August 20, 2001, it stated that "This contract is conditioned on the Superintendent's obtaining and providing a valid and appropriate certification...to act as Superintendent". "The Superintendent will obtain a temporary authorization needed within 30 days of the effective date of this contract." "...failure to provide necessary certification shall render the contract void". Dr. Stripling never became certified to serve as a Superintendent. Perhaps to avoid potential legal challenges, she took the test for certification on February 26, 2005, six months after she retired in 2004.

The investigation report on the false reporting of dropout data ,designed to control damage and ordered by Dr. Stripling cost the district over $57,000 and was completed in 2003. The documented evidence, an investigation by the Texas Education

Agency and local media reports led to major national news stories on the dropout scandal at the HISD.

The report ordered by Dr. Stripling cost the district over $57,000 and was completed in December 2003. The documented evidence and local media reports led to major national news stories on the dropout scandal at the HISD. After the national news media reported on the scandal, Dr. Stripling announced her resignation as superintendent in the spring of 2003.

I met with David Raziq, (producer of the Channel 11 News, undercover portion) about seven times between November 2002 and January 2003 at a restaurant close to my house. I provided evidence that leaver codes had been falsely changed and that the school was reporting zero dropouts. I provided names of dropouts he could interview. I recommended how he could report the story to the public. I declined his request to appear on camera. He arranged to have his reporter interview the principal in her office. On camera she stated that the school had zero dropouts. She did not come across as believable on camera.

The television station completed four reports on the dropout issue, beginning on February 10, 2003. The reporter, Anna Werner, called the report "Houston Disappearing Dropouts". The reports provided evidence that Sharpstown High School had changed its data to reflect zero dropouts. On the day of the first news report, the Dr. Wichmann sent an email to all her teachers and staff informing them of the news report.

In her email she told the teachers and staff that "if there were any errors in the reporting, it would have been a human error, a clerical error". The district response was that they would immediately begin an investigation of the allegations made by Channel 11. The first thing that the district attempted to do was to find out who leaked the report and punish them. I was not a suspect, initially. I had a fantastic relationship with the principal and she was aware that I did not have access to or knowledge of leaver codes and dropout reports.

Kenneth Cuadra, the school technologist, was suspected of being the leak and was blamed for falsifying the dropout reports by changing leaver codes. He was removed from the building within 48 hours of the news reports. He met with the district's investigators and was asked many questions. They soon realized that he was not the whistleblower and attention began to focus on me.

On February 21, 2003, I was interviewed by the district's investigator. I was advised by the president of the Houston Association of School Administrators (HASA), not to provide any information to the investigator. The HASA president had previously served as a senior administrator in the district for over 30 years and was a personal friend of Dr. Stripling. It was his goal to help with damage control by demanding I remain silent during the investigation. However, I provided a written report on the details of the scandal at my interview with the district investigator. The district investigator did not want to take my written report because he too wanted to help control damage and my report incriminated the district. However I insisted that he accept my report.

I knew I would soon be transferred so began removing personal items from my office on February 27th. On February 28, 2003, I sent a very long and detailed email to Anne Patterson that provided information on the issue that only the whistleblower would know. Later in the day she responded with a letter, removing me from the campus and directing me to report to the district office for duty.

When I reported to her for duty, I asked her what my duties would be. She asked if I had a laptop. When I responded "yes", she told me to stay busy with my laptop. Anne Patterson enjoyed working on damage control. She immediately attempted to frame me for all the dropout problems at Sharpstown. She informed the press that I had shredded over a hundred boxes of documents that could prove that Sharpstown had not lied about the dropout problem.

In the Houston Chronicle editorial page on June 18, 2003, an article was published entitled, "F for Effort: HISD's reputation shredded along with dropout records". I was being blamed in the media for the crisis. She began an investigation into the shredding of documents with the goal of destroying my credibility. She arranged for a letter of reprimand to be given to me by the district in September 2003 to again damage my credibility.

Fortunately, I had two witnesses to the shredding of report cards and teacher evaluation reports that I had supervised in October 2002. The witnesses testified under oath that the documents in question were documents that covered discipline and progress reports from the late 1990's. I also had copies of district forms, which were a requirement for authorizing the shredding of documents, which proved what had been destroyed. Anne Patterson knew that I had not destroyed dropout records but allowed the press to believe that I had. Eventually, she failed in her attempt to divert attention away from the dropout scandal and had to retract her letter of reprimand to me.

I was given an office in the area superintendent's office, which was not standard practice. Normally, teachers and administrators who are pending disciplinary action sit in one room. The purpose of providing me a private office was to keep me isolated from everyone else. I used the time to conduct research and to write several editorials that were published by the Houston Chronicle.

On May 18, 2003, I sent a letter requesting that the TEA question me concerning their investigation. I pointed out that a Houston Chronicle article had falsely reported that no one had intentionally altered documents. The agency never questioned me prior to providing their report on August 7, 2003, which vindicated me. One of their findings was that the district under-reported dropouts by 2,999 students.

On May 21, 2003, I also wrote a letter to the Harris County District Attorney's Office asking them to investigate what I believed to be a crime, falsification of government documents by the district. I called and demanded acknowledgement of my letter as I felt they would deny I had ever sent it to them. I received an acknowledgement, however, when their investigation began in 2005, they could not locate my letter.

On June 2, 2003, I sent a letter to the TEA requesting that they investigate the manipulation of attendance records at Sharpstown High School. I provided evidence that students had stopped attending school in August 2002, but were not removed from the rolls until after October 23, 2002.

Dr. Wichmann had kept them on the rolls until then so that the school would qualify for funds provided per student on what is termed the "snapshot day". My complaint pointed out that this was a crime and required investigation. I received a letter from the TEA advising me that they had closed the report on my complaint on June 18, 2003, and adding that they were not required to investigate all complaints.

District Superintendent, Dr. Paige discussed terminating my employment with the district's legal counsel. However, they decided to wait because I had already filed complaints with the Equal Opportunity Office and others complaining of retaliation for blowing the whistle. In late 2003, after a few months of being confined to the area district office, I was transferred to Ashford Elementary School, which served grades pre-kindergarten to the 2nd grade. My duties were very limited. I was to manage assigning lunch cards to students, placing traffic cones in the street by 6:00 am, and performing other menial duties, such as setting up tables for lunch. I am sure they hoped I would resign out of frustration caused by having to perform menial duties with toddlers.

I underestimated the response of the media to the dropout scandal. Soon there were many reporters at my home asking questions and wanting an interview on camera. The first reporter, Ed Lavandera, was from CNN Headline News. As he questioned me on the scandal, he would stop the camera and coach me on what I should say. He instructed me to blame President George W. Bush, who was campaigning for re-election on the basis of his success for the "Texas Miracle" he had created as Governor.

At the time, I was not aware of the president's involvement in covering up the dropout crisis when he was governor, so I refused to talk about the president in the interview. In hindsight, I wish I had addressed the president's involvement in concealing the dropout crisis in Texas. I could potentially have made a difference in the outcome of the election.

In late June, three reporters from The New York Times interviewed me and wrote a series of articles on the dropout scandal and also on another scandal concerning the falsification of discipline reports in the district. The New York Times published a front page story on July 11, 2003, concerning the dropout scandal that contained some information they obtained from me. Soon after that article appeared, a reporter whom I had never heard of showed up at my door and interviewed me for several hours. I later learned the reporter was Mike Winerip, the most respected education reporter in the nation.

On August 13, 2003, he published a powerful article on the scandal in The New York Times. The article reported on my efforts to expose the district for making false reports on the number of students who dropped out of schools. That article was followed by a front page story in Education Week on September 24, 2003. This weekly publication is sent to almost every school and college in the nation. The title of the article was, "Houston Case Offers a Lesson on Dropouts". The article carried a picture of me on the front cover of the magazine defiantly standing in front of the school.

PBS had a weekly news program titled "NOW with Bill Moyers". The interviewer and staff showed up at my house and conducted an in-depth interview on camera. They also visited Ashford Elementary, the school I had been assigned to after completing my sentence at the district office.

The principal directed me to remain in my office with the door closed if the media showed up. I advised the PBS staff to go to the school at 5:30 am when it would be dark and I would be performing my assigned duty of placing traffic cones in the street. The PBS report that was watched by millions was very effective in helping to explain to the public what was going on in Houston with the dropout scandal. The television news report began with footage of me placing cones in the street at 6:00 am. The 15 minute report aired on October 17, 2003.

After a few months at Ashford Elementary School, I became aware that they were in violation of district policy by not reporting discipline infractions by students into the district discipline management records. Most elementary schools practice this policy so that reports show that they have few discipline problems thereby encouraging parents to enroll their children. The principal, who had been the principal for over 20 years at that school, was very unpopular with the teachers. If she learned that a teacher had been talking to me, she would call in the teacher and make veiled threats. In January 2004, I made several reports to the district concerning her false reports of discipline infractions. She soon requested that I be transferred.

I had filed many grievances with the district concerning how they handled my employment. There were several levels of hearings concerning grievances I filed with the district that culminated with a hearing at the school board. My hearing with the board was held on January 14, 2004. At the hearing, I presented my case and answered questions from board members.

One of the board members, Harvin Moore, asked me the following question: "You claim you were working in a hostile environment, but in the CBS report you said you loved your job? How can both of those statements be correct?" I responded by giving an example to the board. I stated that when I served two tours of duty in Vietnam in combat, I was in a hostile environment; however, I had loved fighting for my country. The board turned down my grievance and upheld the administration's actions taken against me.

After the hearing, I was transferred to Sharpview Elementary School. The students ranged from preschool to the 3rd grade. The school was created to improve ratings in the district by hiding low performers. Every one of the 100+ students had limited English proficiency. The school was not authorized a dean because of its small enrollment. However, I was sent there while the district was figuring out how to terminate my employment, legally. The school was housed in a Buddhist temple. The district had contracted to use part of the temple to house and hide Sharpview Elementary School.

My office space was a small closet, which was approximately 4 feet deep and six feet wide. The entrance to the closet was only 24 inches wide and there was no door. The wall had an electrical box with exposed wires. I was given a child's chair and desk to use. My duties were to counsel students (aged three to seven), on proper behavior in the classroom, read to students, and write informal evaluations on teachers during class visits.

Most of the students and teachers did not understand English. Teachers taught in Spanish. Almost all the teachers were recent immigrants from Mexico. One student I met had been at the school for three years and could not speak English. The principal directed me to work on repairing a very large sandbox. I ended up shoveling a lot of dirt and had a picture taken of me performing that duty, which I planned to use as evidence in a lawsuit against the district for retaliation.

The district was making every effort to humiliate me so that I would quit. I decided to file a whistleblower lawsuit against the district in April 2004. While the lawsuit was in progress, I continued my media blitz to help the community understand the dropout crisis in the district.

While I was working at Sharpview Elementary School, the health of my 90-year-old mother was deteriorating. I had visited my mother often and had long talks with her concerning her health and funeral arrangements. She wanted as many of her children to be at her funeral as possible. She wanted to have a service at the funeral home, at a Catholic church and at the gravesite. I arranged everything she requested with a local funeral home.

However, three of her children chose not to attend the funeral. She passed away on May 14, 2004. It was a well-organized funeral that she would have loved. The funeral home did a great job in preparing her remains. The service at St. Patrick's of Nashua was very emotional for everyone. She was well-loved by her family and friends. Jim and Kathryn joined me at the funeral. Afterwards, I returned to Houston to continue my involvement in the Sharpstown scandal.

The producers of CBS 60 Minutes II had also contacted me and wanted to do an interview on the dropout scandal. Dan Rather, the longtime anchor of CBS Evening News decided to conduct the interview at my house. He showed up after all the cameras were setup, the living room prepared and after his makeup assistant had arrived. PBS and CBS provided an in-depth report of the dropout scandal in Houston that reflected poorly on the district and the President of the United States.

The CBS interview was aired on January 7, 2004. An estimated 17 million people viewed the report that night. The interview was also shown on flights around the country as part of an arrangement between the airlines and CBS News.

After I filed my lawsuit in April 2004, the district wanted a way out of the damage they had inflicted upon themselves during the dropout scandal. They requested that we begin negotiations for a settlement. I did not want to settle but neither did I want to be involved in a lawsuit that would take many years to resolve. I felt there were better things to do with my life than be totally consumed with a lawsuit for years. A friend had just settled a lawsuit with the district that had been going on for five years. I did not want to go through what she went through. I decided to accept the settlement offer and $90,000.

As part of the settlement, I insisted that the letter of reprimand given to me in September 2003 be withdrawn. They attempted to contest that requirement but gave up when I said it was non-negotiable. I had done nothing wrong. The letter of reprimand was totally unjustified and meant only to discredit me. I agreed to their request that I resign from the district. The final terms of the lawsuit were signed on June 2, 2004, and my resignation from the HISD became effective on that date. Anne Patterson, the area superintendent was given a letter of reprimand for her lack of supervision. Dr. Wichmann, the principal, was forced to retire and fined two weeks' pay. The associate principal (who was the person most directly responsible for reporting zero dropouts) received only a letter of reprimand. Seven years later, the associate principal was promoted to a high level administrative position in the district that paid over $100,000 a year.

The period between November 2002 and June 2004 was very rewarding because I believe I was making a difference that would have an impact on children. After the media blitz on the dropout scandal, many states around the country began studies on how they reported dropouts and discussed plans to deal with the crisis. However, these were also challenging and stressful times for my family.

During those two years, I was constantly supported, encouraged and mentored by HFT Representative Rosemary Covalt. She became a very close confidante and friend who always worried about me during those challenging times. She visited me on an almost weekly basis at the various schools to which I was transferred. She attended every grievance hearing. She met with my supervisors and reprimanded them for the way they were treating me. She advocated for me with school board members and senior administrators.

Rosemary had a lifetime of experience of being an advocate and working with the media and elected officials. She was truly a very effective change agent whose guidance throughout the Sharpstown scandal was instrumental in my success in bringing about change. I have a deep sense of gratitude for her guidance and support during the Sharpstown scandal and the support she would provide when I was confronted with a SLAPP lawsuit in 2007.

Kenneth Cuadra was a victim of the Sharpstown scandal and suffered immensely along with his family. He was charged by the Harris County District Attorney for altering student records and had to undergo several years of being harassed, intimidated and forced to defend himself. In my view, Kenneth Cuadra was the champion of the Sharpstown scandal, in that he was the first person to reveal that the district was cooking the books on the number of high school dropouts. As a result of his actions, the district's crimes against children were revealed and its reputation seriously damaged. Kenneth Cuadra's courageous actions cost him his job, unfair criminal charges, and many stressful years fighting to regain his reputation. Fortunately, the charges against him were dismissed for lack of evidence.

Sharpstown High School, Houston, TX, 2003. Assistant Principal
(Author) at the site of the Dropout Scandal.

Author's home, TX, 2004. Author and CBS News Anchor Dan
Rather, preparing for a 60 Minutes story on President Bush and his
so-called Texas Miracle, which was based on falsified dropout data,
as evidenced by the Sharpstown Dropout Scandal.

CHAPTER TEN

University Teacher and Community Activist (2004-2007)

From 1975 to 1978, I had served as an assistant professor at the University of Houston while serving with the U.S. Army. In 2004, because of my teaching and educational leadership experience I was encouraged to apply for a vacant position as assistant professor of Educational Leadership at the University of Houston-Clear Lake (UHCL). One of the primary missions of the UHCL is to serve graduate students.

In academia, young and recent graduates with doctoral degrees are recruited to fill assistant professor positions. They are recruited when they are about 28 years old and often teach until they retire. They rarely have the opportunity to gain meaningful work experience in their field of study. Often, all of their instruction in their field is based on what they have read, rather than what they have experienced.

I was scheduled for an interview with the associate dean and a department chair, both of whom had many years of teaching experience, but no work experience in their field of study or instructional area. They made light of my earlier publications because they were published in military journals. They were also critical of my university teaching experience because it dealt with military instruction. They wanted a young doctoral graduate for the assistant professor position and not a senior citizen with experience in the instructional area. They

182

offered me a position as a lecturer, which I accepted with the understanding that I would not have to commute each day, as UHCL was about 40 miles from our home in Houston. We agreed that most of my classes would be held at the University of Houston campus in Katy, which was only 10 miles from our home. I was scheduled to begin teaching graduate students in January 2005.

All the students in my class were working teachers who had enrolled in a program that led to a Master's degree in Education and Mid-Management certification. The degree and certification were required to apply for a principal job in any school district in Texas. Every student in my classes aspired to a career as an administrator, either as a vice principal or principal.

The subjects I taught were finance, leadership, evaluation of teachers, and Texas education policies and procedures. Each class met for three hours a day, usually from 4:00 pm to 7:00 pm. Some of the classes were held in high schools in the immediate area. In the first semester, 15-20 students were enrolled in my classes, which is excessive for a graduate class. Students began sharing their learning experiences in my classes with other students. They informed me that they felt they were learning how to perform the duties of a school administrator from someone who had years of relevant experience. In the fall of 2005, more students began enrolling in my classes and fewer with other teachers. My classes went from 15-20 to 30-40 students, which is unrealistic for a graduate class.

At the beginning of each course, I would provide the students with an agenda, a schedule, and the course requirements. I also provided my policy on absences, which was demanding because students lost one percentage point of their final grade with each unexcused absence. Sometimes, upon hearing of the course requirements and class policy, some students would drop my class. They explained to me that their work and family responsibilities would not allow them to be successful in my class.

One of the final courses each student had to complete was an internship. Each student was required to develop a project with his or her principal, prepare a portfolio that detailed the progress of the project and complete other required tasks. I would to visit the student and his or her principal at their school and discuss the project with them both. The student was required to attend only two classes during the entire semester. The requirements for the course were not difficult. However, several students failed the course and the program because they did not complete all the requirements for their portfolio.

In 2005 while I was teaching at UHCL, we decided to build a large house with a swimming pool in Fulshear, Texas. We believed that we needed a larger house for our growing family. While we were moving in, a local affiliate of Fox News contacted me and requested an interview to follow up on the Sharpstown dropout scandal that had occurred four years earlier and to discuss what had happened since the scandal and my future plans. The news feature would focus on "Where Are They Now?" The news team traveled to our house in far west Houston to film the feature and aired the story on the morning news the next day.

In 2006, we sold our home in Belton, Texas, which we had owned for seventeen years and purchased another house in Tulsa, Oklahoma. Vyone wanted to be near our grandchildren in Oklahoma and to help our daughter with their care. Soon after purchasing the house in Oklahoma, we decided that we did not need the large house in Fulshear and sold it in 2007. We built a smaller house close to Katy, so that I could continue my advocacy work with civil rights organizations in Texas.

I was concerned about the ever increasing sizes of my graduate classes at UHCL. At one point, the university allowed 45 students to enroll in one of my classes. Universities realize a huge income from graduate students compared to undergraduates because of the higher tuition. It is also prestigious for a university like UHCL to have a large graduate enrollment. I became disillusioned with what the university expected of its teachers and students. The Education Department at the University began dictating the curriculum and discouraged us from teaching what we believed students needed to learn to be effective school leaders. When large numbers of students were placed in my classes in the fall of 2006 and more restrictions were placed on the content of my classes, I decided it was time to end my teaching career and become a full-time community activist.

I wanted to have more time to advocate for minority students, conduct research, write, and travel. I officially retired for the second time in January 2007 through the Teacher Retirement System of Texas (TRS). After our decision to fully retire from income-producing employment, we traveled frequently. We participated in cruises, long road-trips, and spent time with family in Texas, Oklahoma, Chicago and New Hampshire. I also continued my research on educational issues and advocacy for minorities who felt ignored by the educational system in Texas.

In late 2006, I had been invited by a professor at Texas Southern University to co-write an article, entitled: "The Equal Treatment of Unequals: Barriers Facing Latinos and the Poor in Public Education" for the prestigious Georgetown Journal of Poverty Law and Policy. The article was published in May 2007. In the 40-page article, I included a page and a half on what I considered to be a lack of performance of a private for-profit educational services company, Community Education Partners (CEP). The corporation had a very lucrative, longtime contract with the HISD and other school districts throughout the U.S. In the article, I wrote that I believed that the schools they managed for profit could be considered "dropout factories". The corporation filed a lawsuit against me on May 29, 2008 for defamation and interference with their business. The lawsuit, "CEP vs. Kimball", eventually demanded over $9M in damages from me. This SLAPP lawsuit would consume a major portion of what was supposed to be my retirement for two and a half years.

LULAC Gala, Houston, TX, 2011. Left to right: Texas State
Representative Carol Alvarado,
Author, Rosemary Covalt, and Former Houston City Councilman
Peter Brown. (Photo taken by Urbanos Bennett, Houston, TX.)

CHAPTER ELEVEN

Challenging a Corporate Bully in a SLAPP Lawsuit (Strategic Lawsuit Against Public Participation) (2007-2011)

I was motivated to conduct research into a private for-profit educational services company, Community Education Partners (CEP) because I believed the company was ruining the lives of a significant number of students. As a high school dropout myself, and having nine brothers and sisters who had dropped out of high school, I had personal experience of the consequences of dropping out of school. Students decide to drop out of school for many reasons, however what caught my attention was schools pushing students out. I believe that the first school where I dropped out pushed me out. There were other factors; however, I believe the primary reason I dropped out was that I had become disconnected from my high school due to the staff exhibiting a total disregard for my education and academic success.

After visiting Houston Independent School District (HISD) "alternative school" campuses in 2003-2004, reviewing articles on the company and conducting research of my own on the company in 2006, I would come to believe that the school district's goal was to push out low-performing or disruptive students by referring them to "discipline alternative education placements" (DAEPs).

After leaving the HISD in 2007, I became more heavily involved with addressing the Hispanic community's concerns with CEP, which had a contract with the HISD worth more than $23M a year. A contract had been in place between the company and the school district since 1998, to provide two alternative schools. Students were referred to DAEPs for behavioral or attendance problems. Hispanic and other Houston communities and I believed that CEP was not providing a quality education for students, and that many of the students referred to them eventually dropped out of the HISD.

My research and the research of others would clearly reveal that almost all of the students referred to the district's DAEPs dropped out of the HISD and perhaps from school altogether. In my view, the DAEPs were contributing to the "dropout factories" identified in the HISD in a study by Harvard University. The term was first used and defined by the Harvard University study on failing schools. I was not alone in reaching this conclusion. The League of United Latin American Citizens (LULAC) also had concerns about CEP being a source of dropouts.

I had decided to become a member of LULAC Council 402 (the education council) in 2002. The group had been criticizing CEP since the early 2000's. As a member, I had begun in earnest to collect information, especially performance data, on the company, in coordination with LULAC members. Our efforts to hold the company accountable for their performance began in 2004 and continued through to 2011.

We learned that in March 2001, the Texas House of Representatives had conducted an investigation of the company in response to concerns from parents of students in the HISD.

The investigation had only consisted of an exchange of letters between the House Education Committee and the HISD. Soon after the Houston investigation, the Dallas Independent School District cancelled its contract with the company (stating it was not cost effective for Dallas).

In September 2004, LULAC Council 402 had requested a meeting with CEP management. They had no interest in meeting with us until we sent a letter to Dr. Saveedra (who had replaced Dr. Paige as superintendent of the HISD in October 2004), requesting that the HISD hold the company accountable and investigate their performance. Soon after the letter was sent, we were notified that senior company officials had agreed to meet with us to address our concerns on November 3, 2004. We offered to provide assistance to CEP in the form of a free consultation service, to help reduce high dropout rates and increase graduation rates. They rejected our assistance. We left that meeting determined to expose the poor educational performance of the company. We began addressing the HISD school board with our concerns at its monthly board meetings. A series of letters was sent to the superintendent and board members reporting on the results of our research. We also expressed our views that many of the students referred to the company were dropping out of the HISD.

In September 2005, an extremely critical article concerning the company was published by a national syndicated journal, The Nation. The article: "Failing Students, Rising Profits" discussed the way that CEP used political clout in the markets in which they operated and how some critics called their schools, "soft jails". The article reported that:

"the few totally independent evaluations of CEP's effectiveness have rated it poorly".

The article quotes an HISD school evaluator who completed a study in 1999. He concluded:

"the longer [students] stayed, the worse their performance".

CEP most likely considered that LULAC Council 402 posed a threat to them. Between May and June of 2006, CEP decided to establish a relationship with LULAC District VIII, which they may have assumed had oversight of LULAC Council 402.

Through their attorney, CEP negotiated with LULAC District VIII to develop a partnership. The company agreed to provide

$10,000 a year to the district for five years in return for the partnership agreement. The HISD superintendent had been convinced by his personal attorney to support the partnership. His personal attorney also happened to be the lead lobbyist and attorney for CEP, which created a conflict of interest. The Houston Press published a short blog reporting that the funds could be considered hush money to silence the criticism of CEP by LULAC Council 402.

Soon after the agreement was signed, LULAC District VIII published a report on its investigation of the complaints concerning the company from LULAC Council 402. Neither I, nor any other members of Council 402 were ever interviewed by the two people assigned to investigate the allegations. They based the report solely on data provided by CEP. The report criticized LULAC Council 402 and me, with the intention of damaging our credibility. (CEP later used this report as evidence in their lawsuit against me. The report was withdrawn by a vote of LULAC District VIII in 2010.)

LULAC Council 402 continued its criticisms of the company, which may have been the reason that CEP stopped their annual payments after the very first payment.

Prior to joining LULAC, I had personal experience with CEP when employed with the school district. In 2003, I had been assigned a special project by the west district area superintendent. The assignment was to serve as a liaison between the school that referred the student and the student who had been sent to the alternative school. I was given a list of 180 students who were enrolled in the program in March 2004.

Two years later, in 2006, under the provisions of the Texas Freedom of Information Act, I requested the graduation or enrollment status of those 180 students. We discovered alarming data that reflected poorly on the performance of the company in serving the needs of students in the district. The data provided to me by the HISD indicated that few had graduated and few remained enrolled in the school district.

We began collecting articles from other states in which the company had contracts. These articles were critical of the company's performance. We provided the articles to HISD school board members, the superintendent and elected officials.

In its fall 2006 edition, another publication, The Notebook, published a negative article on the performance of the company in Philadelphia, PA. The article: "CEP mystery, many pass through. And then?" reported that the company was being paid $28M a year to provide DAEPs for 2,000-3,000 students in Philadelphia public schools. The district's CEO is reported to have called the outcomes, "unmitigated disasters" with zero graduation rates, 50 percent attendance and "pitiful test scores".

We (LULAC) took our data to the Texas Senate Education Committee, and addressed them on our concerns with DAEPs in general, and CEP specifically. On October 4, 2006, I addressed the Texas Senate Education Committee and requested that the committee hold the company accountable, since the HISD refused to investigate. I also provided them information that indicated that 90 percent of students referred to CEP in my limited study withdrew from the HISD after two years.

The Houston Press, a local newspaper, had been writing negative articles about CEP since 2001 and continued to do so in 2006, with a report that included the results of our study into what had happened to the 180 students that were enrolled in 2004. The Houston Press article was published on October 5, 2006.

The next day, the superintendent of the Palm Beach School District sent a letter to the company announcing its plan to terminate its contract with CEP because of:

"multiple serious incidents impacting students' health, safety and welfare . . . ."

The letter adds,

"Despite the fact that the CEP program is built around implementing a successful behavior intervention program: such behavior intervention program appears to be non-existent".

On October 7, 2006, I sent a letter to the Commissioner of the TEA requesting that she investigate the discrepancies in the data reported by the company, the district and myself.

On October 9, 2006, I sent another letter to HISD board members and the superintendent along with a copy of my study and, again, requested that they conduct an investigation into the company's performance.

On November 16, 2006, in response to an invitation, I addressed the full committee of the State Board of Education (SBOE) in Austin. My presentation focused on the dropout crisis and how DAEPs contribute to it. The HFT president (who earlier that year had testified to the Texas Senate Education Committee that she was the protector of CEP) attended the meeting. Two senior CEP leaders and other representatives attended and spoke at the meeting.

The official policy of the SBOE is that speakers who were not invited to speak are given only three minutes to address the board. However, the Deputy Commissioner of the Texas Senate Education Committee (who appeared to be responsible for the time-keeping) allowed them to speak longer. As a result, CEP representatives spoke in excess of twenty minutes defending their company. The Deputy Commissioner (now Commissioner of Education) is a personal friend of the HFT president. In my view, this was another example of CEP using politics to gain favor and support.

In December 2006, LULAC Council 402 held its monthly meeting and voted on a motion to send a letter to LULAC District VIII requesting that it terminate its partnership agreement with the company. The motion to send the letter was approved and the letter was sent on December 15, 2006.

On January 8, 2007, a letter was sent to the Texas Commissioner of Education requesting information as to why the company had not been evaluated in accordance with the Texas Education Code (Chapter 37m and n). Another letter was sent on January 9, 2007 to the Inspector General of TEA requesting the same information. On February 15, 2007, the Texas Commissioner of Education responded and stated that

House Bill 3459, passed in 2003, limited the agency's oversight of DAEPs.

In the spring of 2007, the article Professor Lupe Salinas and I wrote was published in the Georgetown Journal of Poverty Law and Policy. Soon after publication, an attorney who served as a lobbyist and attorney for CEP met with Professor Salinas. The attorney also happened to be a longtime friend and former associate of Professor Salinas. The attorney demanded that Professor Salinas notify the Georgetown Journal that my data was inaccurate and to denounce my contribution to our article.

The attorney left the meeting indicating that the company was planning to file a lawsuit against me and possibly the professor. The attorney followed up the meeting with a letter to Professor Salinas that included threats to damage the professor's career if he did not follow the attorney's recommendations.

On April 18, 2007, a letter was sent to the superintendent and Houston school board members with attachments that provided evidence that there was no oversight of CEP and again requested that they conduct a study of the company's performance. Another letter, with a copy of the Georgetown article, was sent to the superintendent and HISD board members on September 5, 2007, requesting that they terminate the contract with CEP.

Our letters were met with indifference. The superintendent's private attorney (representing his contract interests with the HISD) was the same attorney who had represented CEP since they began doing business with the HISD. The superintendent privately stated to me that he did not learn of the attorney's relationship with CEP until after he had signed the contract for representation. He understood that it was a conflict of interest.

We believed that the superintendent's association with the company's attorney was inappropriate and contributed to his decision not to conduct any review or investigation of the company. One of the HISD board members, who had always defended the company, had previously been a paid consultant for CEP while he served as an HISD board member and president of the HISD school board. As a result of these relationships, there was no action taken by the HISD superintendent or board members in response to our many letters and public addresses made to the board.

On March 11, 2008, the American Civil Liberties Union (ACLU) filed a lawsuit against CEP and the Atlanta, Georgia public schools. The lawsuit author stated that:

"The appalling performance of Community Education Partners is matched by the dereliction of the city of Atlanta in its duty to provide students with an adequate public education".

According to the ACLU:

"CEP's record nationwide is similarly poor and suggests a political strategy to win contracts and increase profits, not a commitment to education . . ."

A staff attorney with ACLU stated that:

"It would be a stretch to even call this a school since there is little to no academic instruction and its students are treated like criminals—it is nothing more than a warehouse largely for poor children of color."

On May 29, 2008, CEP followed up their threats by filing what I believe was a frivolous lawsuit against me, for defamation and interference with their business.

The lawsuit alleged that I:

"launched a malicious and defamatory campaign to end CEP's partnership with HISD and ruin its national reputation as an educational leader clearly stems from his deteriorating relationship with HISD . . ."

The lawsuit went on to say that I:

"published the words and statements with malice; that is, Defendant knew his statements were false or acted with reckless disregard for whether the statements were true, acted with ill will, and/or intended to interfere in CEP's economic interest. Defendant's false statements caused injury to CEP . . . ."

I believed that all the actions I had taken regarding CEP were protected by the first amendment to the constitution, regarding freedom of speech. The constitution grants each person the right to participate in government and speak freely on public issues. Since the company was being paid with tax dollars, LULAC members and I felt that we had the right to address what we felt was the inefficient use of our tax dollars. In 1999, the company was given $21M by the Texas Growth Fund (TGF), which is an organization that was funded with pension funds from the Teacher Retirement System of Texas (TRS). As a beneficiary of the TRS, I also felt I had a vested interest in how those funds were used. The TGF (according to its CEO) owns 80 percent of CEP, which conducts business in many states.

The trial date was set for March 29, 2009. However, no monetary damages were declared. It appeared that the company was planning to use any damages they may incur if the HISD did not renew their contract in March 2009.

I welcomed the lawsuit. It would provide me the opportunity to prove what I had been writing and saying about the company since late 2004. The lawsuit was filed and assigned to the 234th District Court in Houston.

It is my opinion that the attorney for the company, in some way, may have managed to influence the selection of the judge who would hear the case. The attorney for CEP was one of the most powerful attorneys in the city and politically well-connected. Although the selection process is supposed to be set up to prevent interference, I have been informed that there is a way to circumvent the policy. The judge selected to hear the case was a Republican and Hispanic. He was and is a colleague of the attorney who represented CEP. They served together as members and leaders of community groups in Houston.

After the lawsuit was filed, I learned something about SLAPP lawsuits. They are legal pre-emptive attacks by large corporations against citizens and community groups that exercise their constitutional rights by speaking out on issues and urging other citizens to address abuses by public agencies. In May 2008, I considered myself a victim of a SLAPP lawsuit (Strategic Lawsuit against Public Participation). The purposes of SLAPP lawsuits are to silence the victims, force them to pay large amounts of their personal funds for their legal defense, bury them in paperwork, consume their time, discredit them and harass them. In most cases, SLAPP lawsuits never go to trial. The plaintiff often seeks to mediate and settle the case prior to the trial. The lawsuit had not yet specified monetary damages, but CEP would eventually demand $9.2M in damages.

In July 2008, LULAC Council 402 sent another letter to the HISD superintendent and board members and included Philadelphia news article that:

"found evidence that only 500 of the 10,000 students who had passed through CEP doors until that time had either returned to regular schools or had graduated".

This report mirrored the finding of my study of the 180 students in Houston.

CEP had been the subject of many newspaper and journal articles over the previous 12 years. Many of them provided information that included reviews of the company's performance and provided data to support my criticisms of the company. CEP never sued any of the writers of those long articles or those who spoke disparagingly of the company at public meetings.

CEP's attorney indicated to Professor Salinas in their meeting with him that I was involved with the ACLU lawsuit and suggested that the article in the Georgetown Journal convinced ACLU to file the lawsuit. The company appears to have considered the ACLU lawsuit as the final straw in deciding to file a lawsuit against me. CEP's lawsuit against me was filed two months after the ACLU lawsuit was filed. It appears that my letters on behalf of LULAC Council 402 to the HISD Superintendent, board members and elected officials between 2004 and 2007, and my public comments criticizing the company were not sufficient motivation for the company to file the lawsuit. The page-and-a-half I wrote in May 2007, published in a 40-page article in the Georgetown Journal in spring 2007 did not appear to be sufficient. The timing of the lawsuit appears to indicate that the ACLU lawsuit and the upcoming renewal of its contract with the HISD were the triggers for filing the SLAPP lawsuit against me.

I also suspect that the decision by the CEO of the company to sue me was partly influenced by a personal friend in Houston. In Houston, she had a reputation for making threats to sue people when she became angry with them. That friend was the HFT president, who had attended the SBOE meeting in 2006; had testified to the Texas Senate Education Committee that she was the protector of CEP;

The lawsuit was filed in May 2008 and the HISD's contract with the company was up for renewal or cancellation in March 2009. The company may have reasoned that they could force me to be me silent by filing a lawsuit, and that the board would, therefore, renew the contract. The HISD board did decide to renew CEP's contract for five years on March 1, 2009, which should have caused the corporation to dismiss the lawsuit since it had claimed that I had interfered with the company's contract with the HISD. Consequently, the company requested a delay in the trial and it was reset for October 2009. It was reset several times and finally set for January 31, 2011.

The damage model for CEP's lawsuit became a moving target. The company decided to shift the focus of the lawsuit to the Austin Independent School District (AISD). On March 30, 2009, (four weeks after the HISD approved its contract) CEP presented a proposal to provide its services to AISD. When the district declined to pursue a contract, CEP decided it was because of my actions and declared monetary damages for their lawsuit in the amount of $4.7M.

I had no knowledge that CEP had proposed or was even discussing doing business with AISD until the night before the AISD board meeting on March 30, 2009. I received an email informing me that the company was on the agenda at the AISD board meeting I had never contacted AISD, never sent them any materials, nor communicated with anyone in AISD. The company claimed that I had interfered with the AISD contract and, as a result, they were entitled to $4.7M in damages.

On two occasions my attorneys requested a summary judgment (which is where a judge makes an early ruling). Both requests were denied. The judge ruled in favor of CEP on our summary judgment requests and also on other requests by their attorneys. I felt that the judge was prejudiced against our side from the beginning. At one hearing, the judge asked the company's attorney, "What if the jury decides CEP is a dropout factory?" The attorneys for CEP just shrugged their shoulders. I believe that this comment by the judge was suggestive of him believing that the lawsuit was frivolous.

CEP contracts with school districts in other states were being terminated as negative information on its performance was developed and published by school districts. In August 2008, the company's contract with Orlando, Florida, was terminated. It would soon lose contracts with other districts, including Atlanta School District, in July 2009; and Philadelphia School District, in August 2010.

We continued to demand accountability from the HISD. On February 26, 2009, LULAC Council 402 sent a letter to the superintendent of the HISD and board members requesting a meeting to discuss the company. The HISD responded with a letter that did not provide an opportunity for a meeting but expressed the board's support of CEP. The letter was signed by the HISD board president, who was the former paid consultant for the company.

In 2009, LULAC Council 402 members met to discuss the company with several elected officials including State Representatives Dr. Alma A. Allen, Dora Olivo, Carol Alvarado and Scott Hochberg. They did not provide any assistance or recommendations to address the concerns of LULAC Council 402 with CEP. Campaign contributions from the HFT may have influenced their lack of interest in our concerns.

As part of the discovery for the lawsuit, we obtained additional data on students referred to the company's schools over a 10-year period. Of 14,772 students who were referred to the company's schools in the period, only 811 had graduated and very few were still enrolled within the HISD.

On July 16, 2009 an article in the Houston Press reported that the HISD had agreed that some of the statistics reported by LULAC Council 402 were correct. The article was discussed by the HISD school board at its monthly meeting on July 16th, 2009 for over 30 minutes. The HISD board members stated that they were concerned about the report and requested the administration provide information to them on the allegations made in the Houston Press article. HISD officials never provided the information to HISD board members, in spite of their promise to provide reports.

LULAC Council 402 followed up by sending letters to the Texas Comptroller and the TEA in July 2009, requesting that they initiate an investigation into CEP. Both agencies refused to investigate. In July 2009, a non-profit Houston organization, Children at Risk, provided a study of dropouts from the HISD. The study found that of all freshmen students enrolled at Sharpstown High School, in the fall of 2004, only 37 percent had graduated from any high school in Texas by 2009. The report called into question how CEP could claim that most of its students graduated when a regular high school in the district managed to graduate only 37 percent of its students six years after being enrolled as 9th graders.

In September 2009, a new superintendent was hired by the HISD. Unlike the five previous superintendents, he did not sign a contract with CEP's attorney to represent him with the HISD. Dr. Terry Grier had served as superintendent at several school districts. He was experienced and a risk-taker. Six weeks after he assumed his duties, LULAC Council 402 members met with him to discuss their concerns with CEP. He agreed that the program was too expensive and informed LULAC Council 402 members that he had already begun reviewing the HISD's contract with CEP. Eventually, he proposed a reduction in the number of slots that reduced the cost of the contract. The HISD board approved his recommendation on June 10, 2010.

The revised contract directed that the number of placements be reduced from 1,600 to 1,200 in school year 2011-2012. The first contract that the HISD had entered with CEP was for 2,500 placements, which was later changed to 1,600 placements. As a result of the contract change in June 2010, the company's contract was reduced by approximately $4.2M. CEP immediately added that loss as damages in their lawsuit against me, which brought the total damages they were seeking from me to $9.2M. Basically, the company was declaring that my actions caused the superintendent and school board to reduce the HISD's contract with them. In early December 2010, my attorney deposed the former superintendent of the Austin Independent School District (AISD) and the current superintendent of the HISD. CEP attorneys were present at the depositions. The AISD superintendent emphatically stated that he had never heard of me, never met me, nor had any communications with me regarding any proposed contract with CEP. He testified that there was no proposed contract between AISD and the company. He explained that the district was looking at ideas and that the company had presented a proposal but that no action or contract was approved.

The HISD superintendent testified that I had nothing to do with the decision he and the school board made to reduce the contract with CEP. My attorney asked him five different ways if I had any involvement or role in the board's decision, and every time he responded by stating that I had no role. He testified that he had answered the question many times and did not want to keep answering the same question.

A few days after the superintendents' depositions, the company inquired as to our interests in mediation. I wanted to go to trial and did not want to mediate. I felt that we could easily win the case and then could countersue for damages. CEP had set up a website in the summer of 2008 that attacked my integrity and credibility. They prepared a video in 2010 that they placed on YouTube that in my opinion was defamatory. The video used part of my deposition out of context to make it appear that I had not been truthful. My attorney had prepared a motion to sue them for damages for the video and for the lawsuit, which I felt was frivolous and that by definition was a SLAPP lawsuit.

However, I reluctantly agreed to mediation. I did it to reduce the stress on my wife and to avoid further expense on behalf of my insurance company (even though my insurance company had been very supportive during the lawsuit and believed it was without merit).

A mediator who was agreeable to both sides was selected and an appointment to mediate was set up for late December 2010. The session began at around 9:00 am and ended at approximately 4:00 pm. Eventually, both sides arrived at a confidential agreement to settle the case. The lawsuit was formally dismissed by CEP in early January 2011.

Soon after the mediation session was concluded, the HISD entered into negotiation with CEP to further reduce its contract with HISD. CEP proposed closing one of the two campuses it managed and reducing the number of placements to 1,000 students. The proposal was approved by the HISD board at a meeting in January 2011.

The civil lawsuit was described in an editorial in the Houston Chronicle as a SLAPP lawsuit. The Chronicle argued that SLAPP lawsuits assault our democratic principles of free speech by attacking citizen participation. The editorial on March 22, 2011 wrote that:

"SLAPP lawsuits are the bully's chosen weapon against democracy. The bullies must not be allowed to prevail any longer in Texas". "In Houston, former administrator Robert Kimball made complaints to the school district against a private company that contracted with HISD to teach troubled children and the company sued Kimball for defamation. Lawsuits such as these are a clear threat to processes that perform an overriding public good by protecting individuals . . . ."

In June 2011, the Governor of Texas signed the "Texas Citizen Participation Act", a law that is aimed at SLAPP lawsuits, which according to the Houston Chronicle, is:

"modeled after similar acts passed in 27 states and the District of Columbia".

Fortunately, I had obtained personal protection insurance to insure me against such a lawsuit, via a rider in my homeowner's insurance policy. I had arranged for insurance coverage in the event that I was ever sued for slander and defamation. My insurance company provided all the funds for my legal defense and would have been required to pay some of the damages, if CEP had been successful with the SLAPP lawsuit, had it gone to trial.

In some ways, the company's treatment of its students was similar to Laconia State School for the Feeble Minded. Both failed to educate their students or prepare them for success. Neither of the schools would permit visitors, except in rare circumstances. When visitors did tour the buildings, they were escorted by several officials and were not permitted in certain areas. The state of New Hampshire closed Laconia State School for the Feeble Minded because of its history of failing to prepare residents for success. I believe that CEP, which was paid over $200M by the HISD over a period of 11 years, should be closed. The corporation has failed students who were, and continue to be, forcefully placed there by a school district determined to improve its rating and maintain the support of taxpayers.

Funeral of Nancy Kimball, NH, 2004. From left to right: Trudy, Marti, Leslie (aka Buddy), Fred, Danny, Larry, Patrick and Author.

Tulsa, OK, 2010. Top from left: Frank Elkins, Kathryn Elkins, Vyone, Author, Jim Kimball, and Debbie Kimball. Bottom row from left: Kori Elkins, Nicole Kimball, Jami Elkins and Cameron Kimball.

Houston Conference on Education, TX, 2010. From left to right: Carmen Nuncio (President, LULAC Council 402), unidentified woman, Author, Houston Mayor Annise Parker, Mary Almendarez (VP, LULAC Council 402).

LULAC National Convention, Albuquerque, NM, 2010. From left to right: Mary Almendarez (VP, LULAC Council 402), Author, Carman Nuncio (President, LULAC Council 402), Randi Weingarten (President, American Federation of Teachers), Herlinda Garcia (Executive Director, Texas LULAC District VIII).

APPENDIX A

Family Tree

June 14, 2011

DESCENDANTS OF JOHN KIMBALL
MEREDITH, NEW HAMPSHIRE

1. A Kimball[1] is said to have lived in Meredith, NH about the time of the Revolution, who had the following children: 1. David 2. John 3. Samuel 4. Benjamin 5. Timothy 6. Sarah 7. Nancy 8. Lydia 9. Polly 10. Betsey 11. Joseph. Of these, there is only a record of the descendants of Joseph. (This information is from the History of the Kimball Family in America published in 1892)
    (NOTE: Ancestors of Charlotte 2ix AND Stephen 2vi below) reported that the ancestor's name, that was not reported in the Kimball History Book was John Kimball (1731-1819) and he was married to Sarah Crosbie.
    Lt. John Kimball of Meredith (Belknap Co, NH) was in Capt Nathaniel Ambrose's Co in Col Welche's regiment which marched from Moultonborough and towns adjoining, 30 Sep 1777, and were joined to the Continental army under Gen. Gates at Saratoga. After the surrender of General Burgoyne, marched with the guard as far as North Hampton in the state of Massachusetts Bay and were then discharged. John Kimball, LT, entered the service 30 Sep; discharged 6 Nov 1777; time 1 mo 7 da, ce 8, 2s per month. [New Hampshire State Rolls])

2. Joseph Kimball[2] born in 1785; married Betsey Smith of New Hampton, NH. He lived in Meredith, NH.

Children[3]

    i.   Thomas Jefferson
   ii.   John, b. _____d. 1857
  iii.   Joseph, b. Aug., 1817; d. Oct. 6, 1888
  iv.   Hannah. b. ____; m. Feb. 10, 1846, John S. Doloff
   v.   Caroline.
  vi.   Stephen Smith, b. 1822; m. Nov. 24, 1847, Thurza A. Doloff; m. 2d, Jan 6, 1876, Dolly McConnell of Plymouth, NH.
 vii.   Charles Lafayette.
viii.   Elizabeth.
  ix.   Charlotte, m. Dec 7, 1851, George W. Pickering.
   x.   Obadiah.
  xi.   Mary Jane.

3. Joseph Kimball[3] (Joseph[2], John[1]) born in Meredith, NH, Aug 1817; died Hopkinton, Mass, Oct. 6, 1888; married Mary_____, born Jan. 13, 1822 died Randolph, Mass., Feb. 29, 1848; married 2d, Oct. 11, 1848, Mary Antoynette Temple, born 1832. She married 2d, March 20, 1890, Charles W. Parker. He was a farmer and lived after his second marriage in Hopkinton, Mass.

Children[4]

    i.   Jonathan, b. Quincy, Mass., Oct. 23, 1843; d. Medway, Mass,
October 27, 1850,
   ii.   William, b. Quincy, Mass., May 25, 1845; d. Sept. 11, 1845.
  iii.   Caroline, b. Quincy, Feb. 11, 1848; m. Oct 17, 1865, Charles McIllen
  iv.   Mary b. Feb 11, 1848; m. Dec. 6, 1865, George A. Ward

v. Leslie F., b. 1853.
vi. Warren M., b. Sept 5, 1854
vii. John Reuben, b. Sept 7, 1856
viii.   Marcus H., b. Aug 22, 1859 d. Oct 26, 1944
ix. Charles J., b. Sept 14, 1860
x. Charlotte L., b. June 10, 1863; m. Jan 8, 1880, Frank Morse.
xi. Silvia M. b. July 12, 1864; m. Aug. 16, 1882, James A. Green of Marboro, Mass.
xii. Clara S., b. March 2, 1866
xiii.Dennis G. b. March 11, 1868;m. Jan 15, Catherine Carver.
xiv.James, b. Aug. 18, 1869
xv. Osmund C., b. March 14, 1871.
xvi.Mabel, b. April 19, 1875; d. Sept 25, 1889
xvii.   Son, b. Oct 29, 1876

4. Marcus H. **Kimball**[4] (Joseph[3], Joseph[2], John[1]) born in Hopkinton, Mass, Aug 22, 1859; married Nov. 22, 1879, Ellen Moran Temple of Westboro, Mass. Resided in Framingham, Mass. Ellen Kimball died Jan. 20, 1895 at the age of 31 of pneumonia/m 2d to Lizzie Warden on Nov 17, 1897, b 1860 in Brookline, NH. Marcus died in Goffstown, NH on Oct 26, 1944 of arteriosclerosis.

Children5

i. Marcus H., b. Jan 21, 1880; d. Oct 8, 1880
ii. Clarence F. b. Oct. 13, 1881
iii. Henry O. b. Oct. 12, 1885. Natick, Mass.
iv. Child, b and d April 11, 1887 Framingham, Mass
v. Leslie Martin, b. Dec. 9, 1889, Framingham, Mass, d. Oct. 25, 1954
vi. Fred Herbert, b. July 9, 1890.

(Note: All the above information was obtained from <u>History of the Kimball Family in America from 1634 to 1897</u> by Leonard Morrison. Published in 1892 and republished again by Heart of the Lakes Publishing, Interlaken, NY in 1982. Another son was born to Marcus and Ellen that was not mentioned in the History of the Kimball family. The book was published in 1892 and their last child was not yet born. His name was Oliver W. Kimball and he was born in 1894. He resided close to his brother, Leslie Martin Kimball, until Leslie passed away in 1954).

The following information was obtained from the descendants of Leslie Morton Kimball). (Leslie stated that his middle name was Morton, not Martin as reported on his birth certificate. He filed for social security on April 23, 1937 and put Morton when the form requested his middle name. He signed it Leslie M. Kimball and stated he worked at the Langdell Lumber Company in Milford, NH. The birth certificates of his children report that his middle name was Morton. Morton is listed as his middle name on his death certificate. It is believed that his birth certificate was in error and should have reported his middle name as Morton)

5. Leslie Morton **Kimball**[5] (Marcus[4], Joseph[3,] Joseph[2], John[1]) born in Framingham,Mass on Dec 9, 1889, m. Mary T. Blanchard from Stoddard NH on Sept 3, 1908 at Hancock, NH. m. 2d to Nannie (Nancy) Smith on. July 19, 1931 in Amherst, NH b. Lexington, VA on March 17, 1914. They resided in Nashua NH. Leslie died on Oct 25, 1954 and Nancy on May 11, 2004. Both were laid to rest in Woodlawn Cemetery in Nashua NH

Children[6]

    i.   Annabelle, b. Aug. 6, 1932 in Goffstown, NH
    ii. Martha Virginia, b. June 15, 1934, Goffstown NH
    iii. Leslie Morton, b. Oct 2, 1935, Goffstown, NH
    iv. Charles Henry, b. May 1, 1937, Milford, NH
    v. Fredrick William, b. April 12, 1938. Milford, NH
    vi. Patrick Richard, b. March 17, 1940, Milford, NH
    vii. Shirley Mae, b. and d. Nov. 11, 1941
    viii.Shirley Agnes, b. Jan 11, 1944. Nashua, NH

    ix. Robert Harry, b. Dec 21, 1944, Nashua, NH,
    x.   Daniel Paul, b. Dec 16, 1945, Nashua, NH
    xi. Nancy Linda Mae b. July 11, 1947, Nashua NH
    xii. Larry Stephen, b. Jan 26, 1949, Nashua NH

6. Annabelle (Trudy) **Nadreau** [6] (Leslie[5], Marcus[4], Joseph[3], Joseph[2], John[1]) b. Aug. 6, 1932, Goffstown, NH, m. June 5, 1953 Ralph Martin Felling, b. Nov. 15, 1921, St Louis, MO, D. April 11, 1992, m. 2d Dec 15, 1974, Ronald Charles Nadreau b. Oct 18, 1928, Nashua, NH. Reside in Coral Springs, FL. (Served with the US Air Force, Veteran)

Children[7]

    i.   Michael Martin **Felling**, b. Feb 16, 1956
    ii. Teresa Marie **Felling**, b. April 18, 1958
    iii. Cynthia Louise Lodge b. June 10, 1961

Martha (Marti) Virginia **Covey**[6], (Leslie, Marcus, Joseph, Joseph, John) b. June 15, 1934 in Goffstown NH, m. Herbert Wesley **Covey**, b. May 10, 1930, d. July 12, 1975 m 2d _____, m 3rd Robert Lang Children born in Nashua, NH. Resides in Nashua, NH

Children[7]

    i.   Hebert Wesley Covey, Jr. b. June 8, 1957
    ii. Daniel Richard Covey b. Nov 4, 1958
    iii. Jonathan Alan Covey b. Mar 13, 1962

Leslie Martin Jr. **Kimball** [6], (Leslie Sr., Marcus, Joseph, Joseph, John) b. Oct. 2, 1935 in Goffstown, NH. M. Aug. 7, 1960, Barbara Smith of Nashua, NH. Children born in Nashua, NH. Resides in Milford

Children[7]

    i.   Leslie Martin III, b. Nov 7, 1961.
   ii. Dawn Marie, b. Mar 12, 1964
  iii. Jeffery William b. Sept 1, 1966
  iv. Shanna Lynn, b. May 7, 1969
   v. Jason Ryan, b. Dec 7, 1971

Charles Henry **Kimball** [6], (Leslie, Marcus, Joseph, Joseph, John) b. May 1, 1937 in Milford, NH, m. Feb 8, 1958 Joan Jezukevich, m.2d March 1963, Denise Duclos, m. 3d Jan 1967 to Phyllis _____, m. 4th in 1973 to Carol Palmer, m. 5th Aug 21, 1981 to Claire Joubert of Manchester, NH in Kenneth, Florida. (Served with the US Air Force, Veteran)

Children[7]

    i.   Richard, b. Nov 9, 1958
   ii. Randy, b. Dec 12, 1959 (1)
  iii. Charles, Jr., b. Aug 15, 1962
  iv. Kathleen, b. June 20, 1961 (2)
   v. Derrick, b. Feb 7, 1967
  vi. Holly, b. Aug 1971 (3)
 vii. Jonathan, b. Oct. 25, 1973 (4)

Fredrick William **Kimball** [6], (Leslie, Marcus, Joseph, Joseph, John) b. April 12, 1938 in Milford, NH, m. Sept 22, 1956, Beatrice W.Killerby, b. Aug 23, 1941 in Concord, Mass. Resides in Milford, NH

Children[7]

    i.   Deborah L. b. Nov 26, 1956; d. 1957
   ii. Kevin W. b. Oct 12, 1957.
  iii. Valerie J. b. Feb 12, 1959
  iv. Fredrick W., b. July 3, 1960
   v. Scott J. B. August 3, 1962

Patrick Richard[6] **Kimball** (Leslie, Marcus, Joseph, Joseph, John) b. March 17, 1940 in Milford, NH m. Simonne Belzil Oct 3, 1981. Resides in Nashua, NH. No Children.

Shirley Mae[6] Kimball (Leslie, Marcus, Joseph, Joseph, John b. and d. Nov. 11, 1941, Stillborn, Fetal anoxemia due to premature separation of the placenta.

Shirley Agnes **Gens** [6], (Leslie, Marcus, Joseph, Joseph, John) b. Jan 11, 1944 in Nashua, NH; m. Ronald Stickney of Nashua NH in 1964. m. 2d Harold Gens who adopted children. All children born in Nashua NH. Resides in Largo, FL

Children[7]

> i.   Martha Virginia **Gens** b. March 15, 1965. Resides in St Cloud, FL
> ii. Shirley Agnes **Smith**, b. Oct 8, 1966 m. Brian Smith b. Nov 26, 1961
> iii. Tamara Kim **Rodriguez**. July 28, 1972. m. Carlos Rodriquez

Robert Harry **Kimball**[6,] (Leslie, Marcus, Joseph, Joseph, John) b. Dec 21, 1944 in Nashua, NH, m. Vyone Anderson of Seaside, Ca on Dec 18, 1966. b. Feb 5, 1943 in Fargo, ND Resides in Houston, Texas (Served in the US Army, Vietnam War)

Children[7]

> i. James Bradley Kimball b. June 20, 1967 m. Debbie Buckles 1993
> ii. Kathryn Penelope **Elkins** b. Dec 21, 1972 m. Frank Elkins 1995

Daniel Paul **Kimball**[6] (Leslie, Marcus, Joseph, Joseph, John) b. Dec. 16, 1945 in Nashua, NH m. 1966, Rena Alexander, m. 2d Patricia _____, m. 3d Mattie _____. Resides in Litchfield, NH

Children[7]

    i.   Lisa Ann **McAllister** b. Oct 23, 1966 m. Michael McAllister

    ii.   Laura Marie **Cronin** b. May 11, 1968 (1) m. Derek Cronin

    iii.   Daniel Paul, Jr. b. Jan 1977 d. July 1978 (2)

Nancy Linda Mae **Kimball**[6] (Leslie, Marcus, Joseph, Joseph, John) b. July 11, 1947 in Nashua NH. Resides in Greenfield, NH.

Larry Stephen **Kimball**[6] (Leslie, Marcus, Joseph, Joseph, John) b. Jan 26, 1949 in Nashua, NH m. Nov 21, 1970 to Diane Chouinard (1) m. 2d to Julie Lamont m. 3rd to Joanne. Resides in Leesburg, VA. (Served with US Army, Vietnam)

Children[7]

    i.   Larry Stephen Kimball Jr., b. Oct 8, 1971 m. Viola

    ii.   Jennifer Ann Kimball b. March 18, 1973 (1) m. Tim Foley

    iii.   Rose Marie Kimball b. Jan 18, 1989 (3)

7. Michael Martin **Felling**[7] (Annabelle, Leslie, Marcus, Joseph, Joseph, John) born in Japan on Feb 16, 1956, m. Oct 10 1981 Carole Roche, m 2d _____m 3d Carol Jones. Resides in Weston, FL. No Children.

Teresa Marie **Felling**[7] (Annabelle, Leslie, Marcus, Joseph, Joseph, John) b. on April 18, 1958 in Santa Maria, CA Resides in Sanford, FL No Children

Cynthia Louise **Lodge**[7] (Annabelle, Leslie, Marcus, Joseph, Joseph, John) born
Santa Maria, Ca on June 10, 1961, m. George Wade Lodge b. Apr 9, 1961,
Chicago, Ill. Resides in McLean, VA

Children[8]

    i.   Kelsey Anne **Lodge** b. July 31, 1992
   ii.   Christe Louise **Lodge** b. July 19,1994

8. Herbert Wesley **Covey jr**[7] (Martha, Leslie, Marcus, Joseph, Joseph, John) b. on June 8, 1957 m. Dorraine Warriner. Resides in Nashua, NH

Children[8]

    i.   Anthony Paul **Covey,** b. May 11, 1975 m. Aug 24, 1997 to Elizabeth McElmurray b. Aug 23, 1975

Children[9]

Alexander Paul **Covey** (Anthony Covey, Herbert Covey, Martha Kimball Lang, Leslie, Marcus, Joseph, Joseph, John) b. Feb 4, 1998
Alexis Covey (Anthony Covey, Herbert Covey, Martha Covey Lang, Leslie, Marcus, Joseph, Joseph,John_. b. April 17, 2009

   ii.   Aaron Jon **Covey** b. Oct. 14, 1979 m. Audrey Siroice July 31, 2004

Children[9]

Hannah Covey, (Aaron, Jon Covey, Herbert Covey, Martha Covey Lang, Leslie, Marcus, Joseph, Joseph, John)b. Nov 7, 2001
Abigail Covey, (Aaron Jon Covey, Herbert Covey, Martha Covey Lang, Leslie, Marcus, Joseph, Joseph, John)b. March 6, 2007

Jonathan Alan **Covey**[7], (Martha, Leslie, Marcus, Joseph, Joseph, John) b. Mar 13, 1962 m. April 18, 1992 m. Nissa Innamorati. Resides in Merrimack NH

Children[8]

    i. Jacob Alan **Covey** b. Nov 2, 1995
   ii. Jordan Alan **Covey** b. Aug 17, 1997

9. Leslie Morton **Kimball**[7] [III] (Leslie Jr., Leslie Sr, Marcus, Joseph, Joseph, John) b. Nov 7, 1961 m. Penny Oak June 15, 1985, m 2d to Kelley _____

Children[8]

    i. Laura Beth **Kimball**, b. Dec 9, 1985

Children

    i. Austin Michael Smith July 26, 2007
   ii. Payton Alan Boucek August 11, 2010

   ii. Leslie Morton **Kimball** b. Aug 10, 1987

Dawn Marie **McDougal**[7] (Leslie, Leslie Sr., Marcus, Joseph, Joseph, John) b. Mar 12, 1964 m. Robert McDougal Feb 8, 1986.

Children[8]

    i. Justin Ryan **McDougal** b. May 9, 1982 (Served with US Marines in Iraq)
   ii. Marissa Marie **McDougal** b. June 23, 1986

Jeffrey William **Kimball**[7] (Leslie Jr., Leslie Sr., Marcus, Joseph, Joseph, John) b. Sept 1, 1966 m. Karen Olson Jan 4, 1986. Married 2d _____

Children[8]

    i. Jeffery William **Kimball** Jr. b. June 19, 1986

Shanna Lynn **Kimball**[7], (Leslie Jr., Leslie Sr., Marcus, Joseph, Joseph, John.) b. May 7, 1969 m. Johnathan Gosselin June 18, 1988.m 2d ____Borst, resides in Nashville, TN

Children[8]

    i.   Johnathan Taylor **Gosselin**, b. Dec 31, 1987 m. Lesli Anderson on Sept 21,2009 Resides Fort Carson, CO (Served with the US Army in Afganistan)

Children[9]

Caleb Andrew Gosselin, (Jonathan, Shanna, Leslie, Marcus, Joseph, Joseph, John b. Sep 26, 2010

Jason Ryan **Kimball**[7] (Leslie Jr., Leslie Sr, Marcus, Joseph, Joseph, John) b. Dec 7, 1971, m. Heather Seazey Sept 1, 1999 Resides in Manchester, NH

Children[8]

    i.   Samantha Lynn **Kimball** b. Feb 27, 1996
    ii. Trenton Ryan **Kimball** b. Jan 18, 2001

10. Charles H **Kimball**[7] [jr] l(Charles, Leslie, Marcus, Joseph, Joseph, John) resides in Penacook, NH, b Aug 15, 1962 m Nancy Greenleaf on 2/2/82 b.11//10/61.

Children[8]

    i.   Charles Henry III b. June 29, 1982 m Pam Campos in Santiago, Chile on 4/7/09 b. 4/4/84
    ii. Colleen Jennifer b. March 30, 1984
    iii. Amanda Anne b.Apr 13, 1986 (m. July 29, 2006, to Eric Kirsch, b. 4/30/84 (Mandi Kimball Kirsch)
    iv. Kassidy Danielle b. Dec 21, 1988

Kathleen Kimball (Charles, Leslie, Marcus, Joseph, Joseph, John) m. Joseph Dykeman on Feb 20, 2010, resides in NH

11. Kevin W. **Kimball**[7] (Fredrick, Leslie, Marcus, Joseph, Joseph, John) Resides in Temple, NH, b. Oct 12, 1957. M. Rose in 1977. No children

Valerie J. **Kimball**[7] (Fredrick, Leslie, Marcus, Joseph, Joseph, John, b. Feb 1959 m. Stewart Garner of Quebec Canada. Resides in St Petersburg, FL

Children[8]

   i.   Tyssa Lynn **Garner** b. March 19, 1990

Fredrick W. **Kimball**[7] (Fredrick, Leslie, Marcus, Joseph, Joseph, John) b. July 3, 1960 m.1st Kristen, Resides in Manchester, NH (Served with the US Army, Veteran)

Children[8]

   i.   Melissa A. **Kimball** b. June 10, 1989 (1)

Children

      i.   Breanna Niccole Stonerock, b. April 8, 2006 (Mellissa, Fredrick, Fredrick, Leslie, Marcus, Joseph, Joseph, John)

      ii.   Allison **Kimball** b. Nov 25, 1994 Mother Jane Smith (2)

Scott J **Kimball** [7] (Fredrick, Leslie, Marcus, Joseph, Joseph, John) b. August 3, 1962. m. Phoebe Wai on Feb 16, 1995. Resides in Milford, NH (Served with the US Army, Veteran)
Children[8]

   i.   Casey **Kimball** b. Nov. 29, 1994

11. Martha Virginia **Gens**[7] (Shirley, Leslie, Marcus, Joseph, Joseph, John) b. March 15, 1965. Resides in St Cloud, FL. No children

Shirley Agnes **Smith**[7] (Shirley, Leslie, Marcus, Joseph, Joseph, John) b. Oct 8, 1966. m. Oct 1988 Brian Smith and divorced. b. Nov 26, 1961 Resides in El Paso, Texas

Children[8]

   i. Brandon Riley **Smith** b. Aug 4, 1987
   ii. Kristy Lee **Smith** b. Aug 27, 1991

Children[9]

Alexander King Smith, (Kristy Smith, Shirley Gens Kimball Smith, Shirley Kimball, Leslie Kimball, Marcus, Joseph, Joseph, John) b. 2010

Tamara Kim **Rodriguez**[7] (Shirley, Leslie, Marcus, Joseph, Joseph, John) b. July 28, 1972 m. Carlos Rodriquez from Puerto Rico and divorced. Resides in St. Hudson, NH

Children[8]

   i. Alexandria Marie **Rodriguez**, b. June 25, 1992
   ii. Carlos **Rodriguez** Jr. b. July 18, 1998

12. James Bradley[7] (Robert, Leslie, Marcus, Joseph, Joseph, John) b. June 20, 1967 m. Debbie Buckles on Mar 13, 1993 b. Oct 19, 1968 Bethesda, MD. Resides in Ft Worth, TX

Children[8]

   i. Nicole Elizabeth **Kimball** b. July 31, 1995
   ii. Cameron James **Kimball** b. October 17, 1998

Kathryn Penelope **Elkins**[7] (Robert, Leslie, Marcus, Joseph, Joseph, John) b. Dec 21, 1972 m. Frank Elkins on Dec 31, 1994. Resides in Tulsa, OK

Children[8]

      i. Jami Rae **Elkins** b. March 31, 1999
     ii. Kori West **Elkins** b. August 24, 2001

13. Lisa Ann **McAllister**[7] (Daniel, Leslie, Marcus, Joseph, Joseph, John) b. Oct. 23, 1966 m. 1987, Kenneth Fantauzzi, m. 2d Michael McAllister. Resides in Raleigh, NC

Laura Marie **Cronin**[7] (Daniel, Leslie, Marcus, Joseph, Joseph, John) b. May 11, 1968 m. Jeff Laporte 1987 m. 2d Derek Cronin. Reside in Naples, FL

Children[8]

      i. Alexander James **Cronin** April 27, 2000
     ii. Carly Ella **Cronin** Jan. 8, 2004

Daniel Paul **Kimball Jr**[7]. (Daniel, Leslie, Marcus, Joseph, Joseph, John) b. Jan 1977 d. July 1978

14. Larry Stephen **Kimball Jr**[7] (Larry Sr., Leslie Sr., Marcus, Joseph, Joseph, John) b. Oct. 8, 1971 m. Viola Resides in Milford, NH.

Children[8]

      i. Marcus Xavier **Kimball** b. Aug. 13, 1998
     ii. Darion Michael **Kimball** b. May 16, 2003

Jennifer Ann **Foley** [7] (Larry Sr, Leslie, Marcus, Joseph, Joseph, John) b. March 18, 1973 m. Tim Foley

Children[8]

   i. Tim **Foley** b. Sep 29, 1996
  ii. Kavin **Foley** b. May 19, 1999

Rose Marie Kimball[7] (Larry Sr., Leslie, Marcus, Joseph, Joseph, John) b. Jan 18, 1989 m. Scott Denommee. Resides at Fort Polk, La. (Scott served with the US Army in Afganistan)

APPENDIX B

Love letter written by Leslie Kimball to his wife

Concord, New Hampshire
Feb 17th, 1943
(State Prison)

My sweet and darling wife,

Just a line to let you no that I am a lot better, and expect to be back to work in a day or two. I received your welcome letter and was so glad darling to hear your leg is comeing along so good. I sure do hope my darling that you won't have any more trouble with it. It is too bad darling that you have so much trouble but you never mind my darling, there are a lots of days, yes darling and years I hope, that we can make up for what we have lost. It will be wonderfull my sweet when we get back together again. We are going be so happy darling, you and i and the children, for I feel sure darling that god is with us, and I just no he will help us. So please my sweek and most precious wife keep up your courage. We must do all we can to make the best of it for i no the children are looking for us to make a home for them. and darling if we stick together I am sure we can make a happy home for them. You darling wife are such a wonderfull wife and mother and when you say you love me darling I believe you. And I honestly and truly love you sweetheart and I love you more every day. You say you are counting the days dear, well I would but makes it seem much longer. I have just 36 more

Sundays darling, if I have good luck. No fooling honey time does go fast in here., just think darling, spring is just around the corner and we will have plenty of pretty days and I hope my darling that you will use them and try to enjoy yourself as much as possible. You sure do need a little sunshine, you poor sweet darling. I only wish I could take you in my arms and comfort you. For that is what you need darling, a nice little hug and kiss from me darling. And not somebody else, but that my dear wife is one thing I am sure I will never have to worry about. You have always been a true and faithfull wife to me. You sure have been wonderfull and that is why I love you so much. I keep looking at you and the childrens pictures and boy don't I long to take you all in my arms. What a lovely looking family you all are. Darling was it awfull cold this week did you keep warm? We kept warm but it is awfully cold. I will be so glad darling when you can come to see me. You said something about going to see the children down in Southboro. Well I hope darling that you won't try it until warm weather. you won't will you darling? I will read that letter to you that mrs witty wrote me when you come up. Please darling let me no when you are comeing so i will have the letter on me. I wrote to dad and he wrote back and said he was doctoring his eyes. I guess he has a hard time writing. He said he and doris are better but he said he guessed she would have to write until his eyes got better. Please write my darling and be sure to let me no how your leg is coming along. I wish I was back to work for it is lonesome sitting here and thinking of you and the children all the time. When I am working, it helps to take up my mind. Well my darling I am still reading the bible and I am sure it is going to do me a lot of good. I never knew before I was such a bad boy. Well my own sweet and darling wife I will have to close for this time.

From your devoted and loving Husband Leslie to the one I love most dearly.

(Leslie Kimball entered prison on January 9, 1942 and was released from prison on May 9, 1943.)

CPSIA information can be obtained at www.ICGtesting.com
Printed in the USA
240798LV00001B/2/P

9 781463 431778